Visual Impact

Creative language learning through pictures

Pilgrims

David A Hill

Longman

Longman Group UK Limited,
Longman House, Burnt Mill, Harlow,
Essex CM20 2JE, England
and Associated Companies throughout the world.

© Longman Group UK Limited 1990

This book is produced in association
with Pilgrims Language Courses Limited
of Canterbury, England.

First published 1990

Set in Linotron 10/12pt Cheltenham

Printed in Great Britain
by Richard Clay plc, Bungay, Suffolk

British Library Cataloguing in Publication Data
Hill, David A.
  Visual impact: creative language learning through
  pictures
  1. Non-English speaking students. Curriculum
  subjects:
  English language. Teaching
  I. Title II. Series
  420.71

ISBN 0 582 03765 4

Acknowledgements
The illustrations on pages 10 and 11 by Victor Bertoglio
first appeared in *Progressive Picture Compositions* by
Donn Byrne (Longman 1967).

Illustrations
Cover illustrated by Christina Brimage

A letter from the Series Editors

Dear Teacher,

This series of teachers' resource books has developed from Pilgrims' involvement in running courses for learners of English and for teachers and teacher trainers.

Our aim is to pass on ideas, techniques and practical activities which we know work in the classroom. Our authors, both Pilgrims' teachers and like-minded colleagues in other organisations, present accounts of innovative procedures which will broaden the range of options available to teachers working within communicative and humanistic approaches.

We would be very interested to receive your impressions of the series. If you notice any omissions that we ought to record in future editions, or if you think of any interesting variations, please let us know. We will be glad to acknowledge all contributions that we are able to use.

Seth Lindstromberg
Series Editor

Mario Rinvolucri
Series Consultant

Pilgrims Language Courses
Canterbury
Kent
CT1 3HG
England

David A Hill

David A Hill comes from a teaching family. Having obtained a BEd from Bristol University he spent three years teaching in state primary schools in England, before moving to Italy to do two years EFL work in a private language school. Following a full-time Dip Ed (ELT) from Exeter University, he worked for Pilgrims at Canterbury for three months. The next six years were spent as British Council Lektor in Yugoslavia, at the Prizren Teacher Training College and University of Nis. During this time he began teacher training, and returned to England every summer, working for Pilgrims and/or the British Council Summer School at Exeter. In September 1986 he moved to Milan to the post of Academic Adviser at the British Council DTEO, and since 1987 has held the post of English Teaching Adviser there, in charge of the Council's teacher training in Northern Italy. He has an M Phil in Applied Linguistics from Exeter University. Besides numerous articles on EFL topics, he has also published widely on natural history, has published a book of poetry and regularly translates modern Serbian poetry with his wife Branka.

Contents

Index of activities

ACTIVITY	LEVEL	LANGUAGE FOCUS
4.10 Colour my picture	Intermediate +	Expressing personal feelings; justifying
4.11 You're a Volvo!	Lower intermediate +	Group dynamics; discussing character
4.12 Desert islands	Intermediate +	Giving reasons; justifying

5 WRITING

ACTIVITY	LEVEL	LANGUAGE FOCUS
5.1 Reading their own writing	Intermediate +	Personal writing; discussion
5.2 A room of one's own	Intermediate +	Describing; justifying
5.3 What's my advertisement?	Intermediate +	Writing advertisements
5.4 News report	Intermediate +	Writing newspaper reports
5.5 Comparing faces	Lower intermediate +	Writing comparisons
5.6 Story making	Intermediate +	Writing a story
5.7 Picture the scene	Intermediate +	Writing a story

6 LISTENING

ACTIVITY	LEVEL	LANGUAGE FOCUS
6.1 Spot the similarity	Intermediate +	Describing; understanding a description
6.2 Which is my bridge?	Lower intermediate +	Describing places; understanding a description
6.3 Match the description	Lower intermediate +	Understanding a description
6.4 Who did I describe?	Lower intermediate +	Describing faces; understanding a description
6.5 Landscape into words	Lower intermediate +	Understanding a description

7 READING

ACTIVITY	LEVEL	LANGUAGE FOCUS
7.1 Text into pictures	Intermediate +	Vocabulary in poetry; reason-giving
7.2 Pictures into text	Intemediate +	Meaning in poetry; revision

8 WARM-UPS AND ICE-BREAKERS

ACTIVITY	LEVEL	LANGUAGE FOCUS
8.1 A-B-C	Beginner	Warm-up; revision of alphabet
8.2 Flash a picture	Beginner +	Warm-up
8.3 Maria's a spoon	Lower intermediate +	Ice-breaker; everyday objects
8.4 Talking point	Lower intermediate +	Ice-breaker; talking about yourself
8.5 I like, I don't like	Lower intermediate +	Ice-breaker, likes and dislikes

Foreword

This book is the outcome of a love-affair with visuals which dates back to adolescence, when I collected pictures from the Sunday supplements and other sources, for no particular reason other than that they were 'nice'. As I moved into teaching, the pictures went with me; they were extensively used in my years in state-school primary work, and then increasingly when I transferred to teaching EFL.

My own passion was fuelled by those within the profession who already knew the value of visuals for generating language in learners, by the support given by colleagues to ideas of mine which I showed them, but mostly by the results I got with learners of all ages when I taught them using visuals.

Any book of this kind is a synthesis of everything the author has seen, done, been told and read. There are some direct sources, and I have quoted these where possible; if there are items in the book which have no source quoted, but which appear to the reader to be derivative of, or even identical to, things other people have done or written, it is not because of any intentional deceit on my part. It stems from either ignorance of the source, or from the quite frequent occurrence that the author also thought of the same thing. If anyone does feel wronged, I would be pleased to hear from them and put matters right.

It is always difficult to decide whom to acknowledge for the birth of a book. As far as this volume is concerned, the work of the 'greats' in the field are seminal to its background: books and materials by Donn Byrne, Alan Maley, Alan Duff, Shelagh Rixon and Andrew Wright; Susan Holden's encouragement in publishing early articles; useful sessions with colleagues at Pilgrims since 1980, especially comments by Mario Rinvolucri, Cynthia Beresford, Rick Cooper and Chris Sion; the reactions of six 'generations' of students in Prizren and Nis, Yugoslavia, crucial in the trialling and revision of much of the material; the 'green light' from successive British Council ELOs in Yugoslavia – Mike Stimson, Tom Southern and John Higgins; and the constant support and constructive criticism of Branka Aleksic-Hill, herself an individual and imaginative user of visuals. Finally, there has been the support of my editors Seth Lindstromberg and Marion Cooper from the moment that the idea for a book began. To all these, thank you; whatever success the book has is due to them; whatever shortcomings it has are entirely due to me.

David A Hill
Milan
February 1989

Introduction

WHY VISUALS?

The standard classroom is one of the worst possible places in which to learn a living language. Realisation of this has led teachers to search for methods and materials which will help overcome the problems of this unhelpful situation. A whole range of inventions – from language laboratories to video cassettes, from magnet boards to armchairs – have been used to try to bring reality to what is an unnatural way of learning a creative, living system of sounds and forms. Besides the intrinsic usefulness of the various types of language-learning aids, their success has also depended on how they have been used by the teacher. If you are not in sympathy with a particular piece of machinery, for example, you will not be able to help the learners benefit from what it offers; the problem is often that the equipment and materials are already given, and the individual teacher has no control over what is to be used. This is just as true of an everyday coursebook as of hi-tech aids such as computers.

In the face of such a situation, visuals are a way forward. By the term 'visuals' I mean the kind of photographic or drawn pictures which are commonly found in magazines of all sorts. Visuals have the advantages of being inexpensive (in fact, they are often 'free'); of being available in most situations (unlike reading passages, they can be taken from local magazines); of being personal, that is, they are selected by the teacher, which leads to an automatic sympathy between teacher and materials, and consequent enthusiastic use; and of bringing images of reality into the unnatural world of the language classroom.

And supposing we do have some sets of visuals, what is special about them within the whole gamut of materials and techniques open to the teacher of English?

Firstly, well-chosen visuals, imaginatively used, evoke an immediate response from learners in any class – a personal reaction which is the vital seed of all meaningful language-learning.

Secondly, visuals are always fresh and different: the format is variable (large for everyone to see, small for passing from hand to hand); the style is variable (black and white photographs, colour drawings, famous paintings, unknown portraits); and the subject matter is a surprise (the learner never knows exactly what is coming next).

Thirdly, visual materials are highly flexible: they can be kept in discrete sets dealing with a particular subject (people, places) or crossed over for matching activities (which people go with which places?); they can be used for almost every aspect of language teaching, from drilling to discussion, from essay writing to description.

The use of visuals for the core of a lesson is something personal for each teacher to experiment with; what is done is limited only by the preparation time available, the visuals to hand and the imagination of the individual teacher. To act as a stimulus for this kind of work, the book presents 44 ideas, with variations, for lessons built around visuals; they are to be found in Chapters 2–8. They are presented in an easy-to-follow format, and are all based firmly upon actual lessons taught. The instructions given are intended as a guide; teachers should adapt them to suit their particular work situation.

Besides specific lessons in which pictures are the central focus, the teacher will find many occasions on which visuals will be useful for just part of the lesson: as a stimulus for writing and discussion, as an illustration of something being read or talked about, as background to a topic, and so on. Some examples of how this might be done are to be found in Chapter 1. Whilst the actual materials used there to exemplify the techniques may not necessarily be relevant to a given teaching situation, the techniques undoubtedly will be.

WHAT VISUALS?

Selection of visuals

Initially, it is important to cut and keep all available visuals. Once you have built up and mounted a basic stock, you can become more selective about what is kept. It is important to remember, however, that pictures which at first seem to have no use can suddenly become an exciting stimulus when linked, for example, to an article in today's newspaper, to other pictures or to a poem which is being studied.

Criteria for the classification of visuals

SUBJECT
The most obvious way of classifying and storing visual material is probably according to the subject matter of the picture. There are, undoubtedly, basic sets of visuals which are necessary for any collection. Many of these categories can be usefully divided up into sub-groups. The following list is a suggested classification of such basic sets:

1 **House and contents** You could divide this set into the following sub sets for easy reference:
   Types of dwellings (terrace, bungalow, semi-detached, etc.)
   Rooms/spaces (bedroom, drive, garden, hall, kitchen, etc.)
   Furniture (bed, armchair, coffee table, etc.)
   Furnishings (curtains, rug, carpet, etc.)
   Fittings (sink, radiator, door, handle, etc.)
   Electrical appliances (radio, mixer, washing machine, etc.)
   Utensils (spoons, saucepan, vase, saucer, etc.)
   Tools (saw, spade, drill, hammer, etc.)

2 The town You could include in this set the following essential subsets:

Types of road (street, dual carriageway, flyover, avenue, etc.)
Types of building (public, private, commercial, leisure, etc.)
Street furniture (street lamp, bollards, traffic-lights, etc.)
Open spaces (park, car park, lake, river, square, etc.)

3 Transport Include a full range of methods of transport – both functional and leisure:

Land: 4+ wheels (car, lorry, van, railway engine, coach, etc.)
Land: 2/3 wheels (bicycle, tricycle, scooter, motorbike, etc.)
Air (jet, hang glider, balloon, biplane, etc.)
Water (liner, yacht, fishing boat, submarine, etc.)
Animal (horse, donkey, camel, elephant, etc.)

4 Clothes Include as wide a range of clothes as possible. You can subset into contrasting pairs: male/female; indoor/outdoor; summer/winter; our culture/other cultures; work/leisure; traditional/modern, etc.

5 Comestibles This set can be conveniently divided into three sections, with numerous possible subsections:

Food (fruit, vegetables, carbohydrate, protein, etc.)
Drink (hot/cold; alcoholic/soft; fizzy/still, etc.)
Smoking (cigarette, cigar, pipe, etc.)

6 Faces (Portraits) Collect a full range of portraits of people of all ages, both sexes, all styles, types and cultures. It is important to separate portraits of unknown people from those of the famous; they are likely to be used for different purposes, as they provoke different reactions.

7 Landscapes Include a full range of 'portraits' of places – seaside, city, farmland, mountain, etc. – built on, wild, with and without water and so on.

8 Occupations Collect as complete a range as possible of people dressed for (if appropriate) and engaged in the work they do. Pictures of special equipment for particular jobs can be a useful addition to this set.

9 The weather and the seasons Include in this set a series of pictures showing all weather types and illustrative of the four seasons.

10 The human body Collect a set of visuals showing close-up details of the various parts of the human body.

11 Animals This set should concentrate on the basic 'common' animals, and is best divided into:
Domestic animals (dog, cat, horse, cow, pig, etc.)
Wild animals (lion, elephant, monkey, snake, etc.)
Also collect pictures of any animals which are particularly associated with the area in which the learners live.

12 Sport Collect a set of pictures depicting the range of sports, and probably a subset showing the equipment used for playing them. It may be useful to store this set in subsets (e.g. indoor/outdoor, team/individual, ball games, racket games, water sports, etc.)

13 Music and dancing Include a wide range of images connected with music and dancing, and divide into subsets:
Instruments (pictures of individual instruments)
Performers (pictures of people playing particular instruments)
Dancing (pop, ballet, folk, waltz, etc.)
Types of music (pictures of concerts – rock, classical, folk, etc.)

14 Actions Collect a set of pictures which clearly show people engaged in a single action (sitting, eating, running, sleeping, etc.)

15 Personal possessions Collect pictures of those small objects which we keep in our handbags and pockets (pens, lighters, coins, stamps, sweets, etc.)

With these fifteen basic sets of visuals you can cover an awful lot of language-learning ground. It is not intended to be an exhaustive list and, more importantly, not prescriptive. The individual teacher must decide what is necessary for the particular teaching situation.

As for those visuals which 'at first seem to have no use', their classification is only limited by your needs and/or imagination as a teacher. My own collection includes sets entitled 'Behind bars', 'Walls', 'Roads', 'Windows', 'Desks' . . . (you will find suggestions for using these sets later in the book).

IMAGE TYPE
Visuals have a variety of types of image, and these can be useful criteria for classification, particularly as some people feel that the mixing of the types acts as a barrier to response. The basic categories would be:
- colour photographs
- black and white photographs
- colour drawings
- black and white drawings
- cartoons

For some subjects it is perhaps useful to have parallel sets in different image types. Faces, for example, presented in each image type, would provide an excellent basis for discussion, not only of the portraits themselves, but also of the power of the different image types, and personal preferences.

SIZE
Another way to classify visuals is by the size of the image. There seem to be three 'key' sizes:

- Large (20 × 30 cm): useful for whole-class work, or when a lot of detail is required in groupwork
- Medium (10 × 15 cm): useful for groupwork
- Small (5 × 5 cm): useful for games and other groupwork activities

THE MOUNTING AND STORAGE OF VISUALS
Mounting

There are three reasons for mounting pictures onto light card or stiff paper:

1 they will last longer under regular handling
2 the distracting reverse of the picture is hidden
3 it is aesthetically more pleasing for the learners

Storage

Sets of visual materials are quite bulky and their storage can be problematic. A cheap, simple and space-saving way of storing sets so they are easily accessible is to put each set into a strong manila gusset envelope (26 × 37 cm, with a 3½ cm gusset is a very useful standard size), with the name of the set written in large letters at the top. Store these in cardboard cartons (a 30 cm cube is a good size), with a list of the sets in the carton stuck onto the front. You can store smaller pictures in shoe-boxes, closed with a lid to allow for stacking; again, the contents should be listed on the front of each box.

CHAPTER 1

General techniques

1.1 DRILLING WITH PICTURES

Despite the doubts of the communicative school, it is widely believed that drilling is necessary to give learners sufficient exposure to new language items. That said, the sort of mechanical drilling popular in the sixties and early seventies, and beloved by believers in language laboratories, is plainly undesirable. At the very least it is stultifyingly boring for the learners. More importantly, it has little relation to future communicative needs. If you use pictures, however, many of the problems explicit and implicit in what has been said above are removed. Consider the following traditional drill:

TEACHER: (model) The businessman walked to work yesterday.
(cue): Carry
LEARNER: The businessman carried his briefcase to work yesterday.

The whole situation is abstract, and the teacher controls the meaning in the exchange; it is patently a vehicle for practising the past simple tense. Now see how it might work if pictures are used:

EXAMPLE 1

Hold up a picture of a businessman walking to work with a briefcase in his hand.

TEACHER: (showing picture) The businessman walked to work yester-
day. Tell me something else he did.
LEARNER 1: He carried his briefcase.
TEACHER: Good; anything else, anyone?
LEARNER 2: Yes. He wore a brown suit.
. . . and so on.

Once you have given the model, there is often no further need for teacher prompting. Another way of working is to have a pile of pictures showing actions and elicit only one response from each:

EXAMPLE 2

TEACHER: (showing picture to give model) The businessman walked
to work yesterday.
TEACHER: (showing picture of two boys fishing to give cue)
LEARNER 1: The boys went fishing yesterday.
TEACHER: (showing picture of girl eating an egg to give cue)
LEARNER 2: The girl ate an egg yesterday.
. . . and so on.

The point is that here the picture becomes the cue and the learner's response involves not only using the structure being practised, but also providing the correct vocabulary for the situation. Plainly the onus is on you to provide pictures which only contain vocabulary for objects and actions which have been pre-taught. In this way you are backgrounded, and you only have to react to the correctness of the response, preferably by non-verbal elicitation from other learners.

So far the examples have shown drills which allow the learners to 'talk about' the picture (i.e. they describe what they can actually see). However, it is far more productive, in communication terms, to set up drills in which the learners can 'talk through' the picture (i.e. they take the idea encapsulated in the visual and relate it to personal experience). (This classic distinction was first made in Corder 1963.) The 'talking through' the picture drill might go like this:

TEACHER: (showing two pictures: meat, fish, to give model)
               Which do you prefer – meat or fish?
LEARNER 1: I prefer fish.
TEACHER: (showing two pictures: cherries, strawberries, to give cue)
LEARNER 1: Which do you prefer – cherries or strawberries?
LEARNER 2: I prefer strawberries.
               . . . and so on.

EXAMPLE 3

The above example is taken from a particular semantic field – that of food – and relates it to a structural pattern. It is equally possible to set up the model as above, but change the subject of the cue pictures:

TEACHER: (showing two pictures: meat, fish, to give model)
               Which do you prefer – meat or fish?
LEARNER 1: I prefer fish.
TEACHER: (showing two pictures: rugby match, soccer match, to give cue)
LEARNER 1: Which do you prefer – rugby or football?
LEARNER 2: I prefer football.
TEACHER: (showing two pictures: plane, train, to give cue)
LEARNER 2: Which do you prefer – travelling by plane or by train?
LEARNER 3: I prefer travelling by train.
               . . . and so on.

EXAMPLE 4

In drills such as those in Examples 3 and 4, one is asking the learners to produce truthful answers. It is therefore important to pre-teach (or teach as the need arises) forms such as *I like them both as much* or *I don't like either of them.*

1.2 ESSAY WRITING

Very often, English department syllabuses include an essay-writing component. Teachers often find this useful at higher academic levels (final year secondary school learners, university students) as a way of focusing on different writing styles and honing the learners' English. In many situations it may also have the more pragmatic role of teaching learners how to pass parts of examinations, or how to prepare for papers (often literature) in other parts of their course.

Although the practice of essay writing is valuable for language development, this is not usually enough to motivate the learner for what is, without doubt, an arduous task. It is important, therefore, to provide an adequate stimulus for the writing task. Traditionally, this has been done by giving the learners a reading passage on the subject of the essay, often with pure language questions after it, and sometimes with points for discussion. This gives the learners the background, leaving them free to concentrate on the organisation of the essay, whether it be reflective, argumentative or literary.

Too much written input can, however, adversely influence the learners. They feel that it has 'already been done' in the reading passage, and react negatively to the language questions. Much of this can be softened by a lively discussion. Much more of it can be avoided by using visual stimuli instead of (or as well as) written ones at the pre-writing stages of a lesson:

EXAMPLE 5

Essay Topic: 'Walls' (taken from the useful lists of possible essay titles given in Alexander 1965)

Essay Type: Reflective

1 Split the class into groups of four or five, and give each group a pile of pictures. Say nothing about the content of the pictures or the aim of the lesson. Encourage the learners to enjoy, discuss, comment on and ask about the pictures. These all show walls of different types. The range is enormous: from the Great Wall of China to a suburban garden wall; from graffiti-covered walls to Byzantine frescoed walls; from castles to houses; of rock, of paper . . . . Each group has about thirty pictures.

2 When you sense that this looking period is over, ask the groups to classify the pictures according to purpose. Give no clues on subject or possible grouping. When it is plain they have finished, ask what the common element is between the pictures. Elicit 'walls', and then allow the groups to take it in turns to explain the groupings they have decided upon. List these on the board. Usual areas are 'walls for protection', 'for separation', 'for decoration', etc.

3 Next ask the learners to re-classify the pictures, using categories not listed on the board. Add these ideas to the list.

4 A discussion may then ensue on building materials, builders, similarities and differences according to time, place and culture.

5 Then personalise the activity by asking the learners either to select a picture which they particularly like (or dislike), or one which reminds them of a wall they know well, or a wall they have seen, and tell the rest of their group about it. This ends the introduction of the topic at the literal level.

6 Now show the learners pictures of people building a dry stone wall; ask them to comment on what is happening and what the problems of the process are. At this stage you could give an optional dictation passage (an adapted text from Arnold 1968 or Mercer 1986, which talk about how dry stone walls are built). This leads nicely on to a reading of Robert Frost's poem *Mending Wall,* which forms the link between the literal concept of walls, and the figurative sense of the wall as a barrier to human communication.

7 Following a discussion of the poem, move on to a listening comprehension exercise based on the Melanie song *Close to it all,* which is entirely about figurative walls. Discuss the meaning of the song, and round up.

8 Set the learners the homework topic of writing an essay on the subject of 'Walls'. By now they have enough background from a variety of stimuli to be able to produce a good reflective essay, taking either the literal or the figurative approach.

This kind of integrated introduction to the subject, with visual and lyrical images, leads to far more individual and creative essay writing than introductions which rely simply upon a reading passage plus discussion. Other topics for a reflective essay which I have treated in the same way are 'Bridges', 'Gateways' and 'Windows'.

1.3 STORY TELLING

The publication of *Once Upon a Time* (Morgan and Rinvolucri 1983) has given a strong impetus to the use of story telling in the language classroom. They have suggested several ideas for using visuals (particularly 7.1 *Photos* and 7.5 *Fire stories*). Their techniques are at variance with the ideas in earlier books (Heaton 1975 and Byrne 1967) which present the learner with a set of pictures showing a number of incidents in a story which the learner is supposed to tell. However, 'anyone with normal eyesight produces much the same story, which robs the telling of any point' (Morgan and Rinvolucri 1983, p. 3).

If you wish to use sequential incident pictures as a base for story telling there are ways around this problem. You can cut up the pictures and give them to the learners who then have to order the story before telling it (see Ur 1981, pp. 60–65 and Maley *et al* 1980, pp. 68–83). Alternatively, you can mix up two or three sequential picture stories which are related in theme and of a similar style:

Use picture sequences 4, 7 and 16 from *Progressive Picture Compositions* (Byrne 1967) reproduced below.

EXAMPLE 6

1 Split the class into pairs or fours and give each group a set of the twelve pictures. Ask them to put them into order – don't tell them that there are three different stories at this stage.

2 The pairs (groups) report back to the class on the orderings they

have made. Allow them to draw general conclusions – this usually means agreement that there are three stories.

3 Ask pairs (or individuals) to tell the story they like best to each other. Any pair which has their own arrangement can tell that story.

4 Then ask the pairs to invent their own story using as many or as few of the twelve pictures in whatever sequence they choose. They should tell their stories to some other pairs.

Composition 4

Composition 7

Composition 16

© Longman Group UK Ltd 1990

An exercise like this one is inevitably fairly heavily guided, because the pictures used are related to each other and were intended to go together in a particular sequence. For freer work the following approach seems preferable.

Use a set of black and white photographs (about 10 × 15 cm) showing people, places and objects. To aid imagination, many of these photos should be out of the ordinary in some way.

EXAMPLE 7

1 Divide the class into groups of four. Each group selects five pictures from the pile proffered by you. Ask the groups to look at them and work together to produce a story based on all five pictures.
2 Moving clockwise, two of each group move on to the next table where they are told the story of the pictures there. They then stay there while the other pair move on. They have to tell the story they just heard to the new arrivals, and then move on. The move-and-listen/stay-and-tell system continues until the pairs who moved first arrive back at their own original place, to be told the story they invented by the pair who are there.

This technique allows the learners to listen to and tell many different stories. Great interest is created by the final stage, when they hear how different (usually!) their story is after going through several sets of ears and mouths. A possible further step is that the original group get back together and discuss the differences between their version and the one the first pair to move have just heard. Also the stories can be taped or written down, and the pictures which went with them noted. These can then be read or listened to later (or used for a sorting activity by another class). Individuals may like additional time to circulate to hear the original versions of the stories they heard on their way round.

(A similar activity is described by Maley and Duff 1978, p. 132.)

1.4 LITERATURE

There has been a movement towards the use of literature in the English language classroom in recent years, helped on by such lucid works as Brumfit and Carter (1986), Carter and Long (1987) and Gower and Pearson (1986). The underlying approach is to ask the learners to respond to the language presented in the texts, and in many ways originates in stylistics. This is fine when the literary texts deal with topics which are within the experience of the learners, but often these works lie outside that experience.

The introduction of the subject matter of the literary text can be done very well using visuals. It is what I have called elsewhere (Hill 1986) surrogate experience, and aims to allow the learners to go through – as nearly as possible – the experience which the writer of the text to be studied underwent:

EXAMPLE 8

Visuals: Colour pictures of King's College Chapel

Other Materials: The poems *King's College Chapel* by Charles Causley and *Sunday Morning, King's Cambridge* by Sir John Betjeman and a tape of King's College Choir

Focus: Appreciation of two modern British poets, with opportunities for comparison and contrast of language, style, approach and attitude

1 Sit the class in a circle (or circles, for large groups), and ask them to be quiet. Play a tape of King's College Choir singing, for example, Tallis's 'Sancte Deus' and pass round colour pictures of King's College Chapel, inside and out.

2 After a few minutes, when everyone has seen all the pictures, fade the music and brainstorm the experience. Write up on the board all the words and phrases given by the learners about what they have just seen and heard.

3 Hand out copies of the two poems. Ask the learners to read them through quite quickly and underline any words in the poems which appear on the board, either exactly, or as a synonym, or as something very similar. Usually a number of the items given by the learners are the same or similar to those in the poems. This is often a pleasant surprise for them, although it should not be, as they have have had a scaled-down version of the experience which induced the two poets to write their poems in the first place. This discovery – *we came up with the same words as two British poets!* – gives a new self-image to the learners, and they tackle the rest of the tasks with an enthusiasm born out of the feeling that they in some way 'created' the poems.

4 The continuation of the lesson depends on what the individual teacher wishes to get out of it: discussion of similar words in the two poems, the different outlook of the two poets, the form used, and so on might well lead on to an essay of comparison. Alternatively, you could ask learners to personalise the experence they had in a building of importance; or they might be given a further 'surrogate experience' (different music and pictures) and asked to write about it. It is up to you.

1.5 DISCUSSIONS

There seem to be two schools in the approach to discussions. One of them expects learners to discuss an important topic (e.g. pollution or abortion) cold, before going on to read a passage about the subject and answer some questions – often language questions. The other approach is where the learners are given a text to read, with questions – again, often language questions – to answer, before moving on to discuss the subject raised in the passage.

Both of these approaches are inappropriate, as each in its own way discourages the learners from free discussion of the topic. The first, because the learners are unlikely to get going on the topic without some sort of stimulus, and anyway the discussion appears to be a thinly disguised way into a reading comprehension passage. The second, because the learners are bored with the topic, and are likely just to repeat what was said in the text.

To counteract these situations, it is useful to use a visual stimulus. It is also helpful to choose a subject which is within the learners' range of experience (e.g. road accidents: almost everyone has seen, been in or knows someone who has been in a road accident), or which has 'current affairs' value (e.g. there has just been an act of terrorism in the news, thus terrorism is a 'live' topic). Discussions are far more likely to take off if informed by real attitudes and direct experience:

EXAMPLE 9

Topic: Road accidents
Visuals: Pictures of a large range of types of road accident (motorway pile-ups; head-on collisions; fires; cars with trees fallen on them and so on)

1 Give each learner a picture, and ask them to look at it and think about it.
2 Then encourage them to look at the pictures their neighbours have, and talk about them.
3 Elicit the theme of the pictures from the class.
4 This established, ask the learners to stand up and walk around looking at other people's pictures. They should gradually get into groups with learners who have similar pictures, and be prepared to explain the reason for their grouping.

5 Elicit the reasons and list them on the board. This is generally a list of accident types and/or causes.

6 The next step is to extend the list of road accident types and causes from the learners' own experience. Put the learners into groups and ask them to tell each other about road accidents they have 'experienced' (first hand – been involved in/seen; second hand – been told about/seen on TV or at the cinema). Ask the groups to list the causes.

7 What happens next is up to the individual teacher.
Useful continuations are:

a discussion: read the latest road accident figures and talk about road accident prevention

b role play: give pairs role cards detailing attitudes of people involved in a road accident

c writing: do a police report of a road accident, providing diagrams and details (see Matthews *et al* 1985, pp. 48–51)

d writing: do a newspaper report based on the pictures originally given out, following the analysis of a real newspaper report (e.g. Land 1975, Unit 9)

e language work: make predictions, using the two before/after wallcharts of an accident (Byrne 1976)

There are various different types of discussion which I have classified below according to the learners' personal experience of the topic. I have also included some examples of visuals in my collection to illustrate what may be used:

a things which I know about, and which I have first or second-hand experience of (e.g. accidents, smoking, drugs, pollution, violence in sport, etc.)

b things which I know about but (hopefully) have no experience of (e.g. terrorism, crime, war, prison, etc.)

c things which I don't know about (e.g. marriage between animals in California, honey-collecting in Nepal, bizarre fashions, etc.)

d impossible things (e.g. a woman running down a street with a giant foot about to step on her, people riding motor scooters surrounded by giant tortoises and snails, etc.)

Type **a** was exemplified above, and type **b** may be treated in the same way; these are the commonest types of discussion used in language teaching. Type **c** relies for success on the pictures, and the surprise and interest generated by them; as the learners have no previous experience of the topic, all discussion will centre around their immediate response to the visual images, and you will need to be careful to follow the points raised, and draw out further ideas. Type **d** requires similar treatment to type **c** as it is the immediate reaction to the impact of the unknown and unusual that has to be harnessed; the reaction, however, will be slightly different, in that the imagination is more likely to be triggered by the 'impossible' situation. A good continuation for type **d** is to ask the learners to write a story of which the picture is the beginning, the end, or a part.

1.6 CULTURAL BACKGROUND

Teaching language is teaching the culture of the people who speak that language, and any authentic materials will have reference to objects, places, customs, habits and traditions which are alien to the language learner. It is up to you to make the meaning clear to the learner in the best possible way. If the explanation is accompanied by a visual image – where appropriate – the learner will understand far better: the picture makes the words more accessible.

So, a teacher targetting on British English should build up collections of pictures of typically British foods (fish and chips, ploughman's lunch, English breakfast), places (pubs, suburban housing, parks, football grounds), people (police officers, fox hunters, people who deliver milk), institutions (royalty, parliament), and so on. Teachers targetting on other varieties of English need collections based on the cultures of those communities. Such pictures may then be used on suitable occasions: when something is mentioned in a text being studied; when it has been in the local news; when it is a special festival (e.g. British Christmas compared to the local one); or as a special topic on its own. The treatment of an angle of the target culture in relation to the same angle of the local culture makes a fine basis for a lesson practising the language of comparison:

EXAMPLE 10

Topic: Houses
Focus: Giving reasons; justifying; comparing and contrasting
Visuals: A large collection of pictures of houses from around the world; half are from the learners' country, a quarter from the target culture country, and a quarter from a range of other world cultures

1 The learners get into groups. Give each group thirty to fifty pictures of houses. Ask them to separate the pictures into two piles: houses from our country and houses from other countries.
2 Then ask them to decide what it was that helped them to make their choices; later, elicit these ideas and list them on the board.
3 Take away the pictures of houses from the home country, and ask the groups to decide which houses they think come from the target culture country, and why. Remove the other pictures, and let the groups compare results and reasons, which you may note on the board.
4 Finally, in pairs get them to choose a picture of a house from their own country, and one from the target culture country, and write a description, comparing and contrasting the two.

This type of activity is one way of explicitly drawing attention to the distinctions between cultures, and is a good exercise to do with topics such as food, dress, people in uniform and buildings.

You can do much to promote an awareness of cultural differences and similarities implicitly by choosing and using pictures which represent the target culture for all types of work. For example, when targetting on British culture, the teacher should have a set of landscape pictures which contains British mountains, lakes, coasts, villages, bridges, etc.; the portraits would only be of British people, and so on. You should also have sets of landscapes with widely different pictures: alps, deserts, coral atolls, ice-flows, with people of different cultures and so on, for comparative purposes. But for everyday work you are helpng your learners far more by using target-culture visuals.

1.7 DIALOGUES

Another type of language practice activity which you can usefully set up with visuals is the dialogue. Often, when you ask learners to get into a role and practise a particular function through a dialogue, they find it difficult, as they cannot relate the type of information written on the typical role card to the interaction required. Look at a role card such as:

You bought a radio in the shop last week, using all your savings. It has not worked since you got it home. Take it back to the shop and complain.

Such a cue often results in a very unnatural dialogue in which, although the exponents may be correct, there is little or no 'character' (feeling, intonation, expression) put into the role. With suitable visuals you can resolve the problem to a large extent.

Instead of just giving the learners role cards with the information on them, give each pair also a picture which illustrates the interaction. In this way they have a setting in mind, and they can also use the expressions and gestures of the people in the picture as a model. This information can be immediately internalised, and goes a long way towards helping them to get into a role.

Another advantage of this activity is that if you have pictures of different types of people engaged in the same language function, the learners can produce interesting work on degrees of formality and register. Open performances by the pairs with the picture displayed can lead to whole-class discussion of the appropriateness of the language used to the situation in the picture.

1.8 ORAL EXAMINATIONS

Cambridge language examinations (FCE, CPE and now PET) have long used photographs as a stimulus during oral testing. Carefully selected visuals make an excellent focus and starting point for discussion in oral examinations. The sort of picture which is most useful is a colour photograph, about 20 × 30 cm in size, showing several people engaged in different activities, surrounded by lots of objects, and in a definable place. Two copies of the same picture are necessary – one for the candidate and one for the examiner:

Suggested oral examination procedure.

EXAMPLE 11

1 Hand a picture to the candidate and say, *I'd like you to look at this picture for a few moments.*
2 After about a minute, say, *Please would you tell me something about the picture in your own time.*
3 Then allow the candidate to say whatever they want about the picture, occasionally helping them with an item of vocabulary, or asking them to clarify something if you feel it necessary.
4 On sensing that the candidate is drawing to a close, you should ask some specific questions about the picture, especially concerning any vital elements which the candidate has not mentioned, and would be expected to be able to talk about at that level.
5 You may also ask the candidate to go into detail on a particular area of language use you wish to test. This is likely to involve the use of lexis and structures taught during the period of language learning being tested, e.g. *Will you give me a full description of what the girl on the left is wearing, please?* or *Can you give me the names of some of the tools which you can see in the garage, please?*
6 The next stage of the test should be to personalise the picture by asking the candidate to express their attitude towards what is happening in the picture, their experience of such events, what they think will happen next, and so on.

This type of questioning technique allows you (the examiner) to assess the candidate's ability in the skills of general description, detailed description, self-expression, prediction, and their breadth of vocabulary.

1.9 NAMING

Naming is, perhaps, one of the more obvious things to do with pictures, but is more or less useful, depending on how it is done. In the same way that the idea of holding up a pen and asking *What's this?*, expecting the answer *It's a pen* is uncommunicative, it is uncommunicative to hold up a picture of a pen and ask *What's this?* expecting the same answer. It is possible, however, to use pictures to check on the learners' acquisition of certain lexical items in a more communicative way:

Hold up a large picture of a table with various items on it.

EXAMPLE 12

TEACHER: Paola –tell me one thing you can see on the table.
PAOLA: There's a plate.

TEACHER: OK. Nella – what's on the left of the plate?
NELLA: A fork.
TEACHER: Right. Maria – what's on the plate?
MARIA: An apple.
TEACHER: Yes. Stefano, the apple's green; what else is green?
STEFANO: The plant is green.
        . . . and so on.

In this way the items are all named within a context, through an activity which involves listening comprehension and understanding of an overall situation (here, objects on a table, their spatial relationships and other qualities); it has more intrinsic communicative value than simply asking *What's this?*.

Where you need a quick check of newly-learnt lexical items you could use the following 'fast naming' technique:

EXAMPLE 13

Visuals: A large pile of pictures illustrating recently-learnt vocabulary. It it helpful if these are from the same semantic field (e.g. furniture)

1 Quickly turn over each picture and get the class to shout out the name of the item of furniture seen.
2 Give the name of any item which has been forgotten and practise it; you can then put the picture on one side and reintroduce it every four or five pictures to reinforce it.
3 Question any learners who are not joining in:

TEACHER: (cues response by holding up a picture of an armchair)
LEARNERS: Armchair.
TEACHER: What did they say, Karl?
KARL: Armchair.
TEACHER: Are they right?
KARL: Yes.
. . . and on to the next picture.

This activity is enjoyable and almost game-like if the teacher keeps it moving along at a good pace.

This kind of naming/revision activity using pictures can be put into a small group framework as well:

EXAMPLE 14

Visuals: A large number of small pictures illustrating recently learnt items of vocabulary

1 Divide the class into groups of four, and give each group a pile of fifty small pictures face down in the middle of the desk.
2 The learners take it in turns to turn over a card and name the object on it. If they know the item, they keep it. If they don't know it, they put the card back at the bottom of the pile. In both cases the turn passes to the next learner.

3 The game continues until the learners have taken all the cards. They are then counted, the winner being the person with the most cards.

4 At the end the learners tell each other and test each other on any items which they did not know.

1.10 DESCRIBING

Talking about what they can see in pictures is another basic and obvious activity for language learners. As with naming, it is more or less useful depending upon how it is carried out. Certain types of visuals naturally lend themselves to this activity as a way of practising a normal communicative situation: describing faces, places and objects are very necessary language skills, closely followed by the description of what people are wearing and what they are doing.

It helps learners if they have a 'formula' to hang on to in order to focus their thoughts when handling new language. It is useful, therefore, to teach logical ways of description: for instance, describe the shape and colouring of the face before details of the size of the nose and the length of the hair; divide a view into foreground/middle/background and left/middle/right. You will find this kind of approach very often in textbooks; use visuals to give practice in the newly-learnt skill. You can do this in a game-like activity which is more authentic communicatively:

EXAMPLE 15

Visuals: Sets of small/medium pictures of whatever it is the learners have lately been learning to describe (e.g. six or eight red cars)

1 Get the learners into pairs; give each pair a set of pictures, which are taken by Learner A.

2 A looks at the pictures and mentally chooses one of them. Learner B must not know which one.

3 A lays the pictures on the desk; B then asks a *Which...?* question (*Which of them is your new car?*).

4 A describes the chosen picture (*It's the one with...*); B listens to the description and indicates which one it is. If it is right, they do the activity again the other way round; if it is wrong, then A describes again.

NB Other possibilities: six or eight people (B: *which of those is your cousin? A: The one with . . .*); six or eight jackets (B: *which jacket do you like best? A: I prefer the one with . . .*) and so on.

The description of action is another frequently used activity. It almost becomes a naming device if you hold up a picture of a woman driving a car and ask *What's she doing?* expecting the answer *She's driving*. This can be improved by expecting the learners to give a full answer to a question like *What's happening in this picture?*. The answer may be of two kinds:

a *There's a woman sitting in an armchair reading a newspaper* (the literal answer to what is seen in the picture);

b *There's a man sitting at a table; he's writing a letter to his friend* (an imaginative answer to a picture showing a man sitting at a table writing something unclear).

It is important to try and get away from the *What are they doing? – They're drinking* mode. Here is a way of doing it:

EXAMPLE 16

Visuals: Pictures showing one action from which another may be easily and logically understood

Focus: *Present continuous/going to* future

Show a picture of a girl, dirty from football, taking off her kit in the bathroom

TEACHER: What's happening in this picture?

LEARNER 1: There's a girl getting undressed.

TEACHER: Why?

LEARNER 2: She's going to have a bath.

TEACHER: Why?

LEARNER 2: Because she's dirty.

. . . and so on.

In this way the language is contextualised; the learners use their knowledge of the world to describe what they see and move on to predict what is going to happen next.

CHAPTER 2

Games

KIM'S CARDS

Procedure

1 Divide the class into groups of about six, and ask the groups to sit as far away from each other as possible.
2 Give each group a picture, which they must now show to the other groups. Ask them to work out fifteen questions about it (you might give them an example or two). Each group should appoint a secretary to write down the questions.
3 While they do this, you should circulate, helping with language, suggesting which are the most suitable questions. Help filter out questions which are too easy, too obscure or too similar to others.
4 When the groups have all got fifteen questions, they should select the best ten, and all copy them down, with the answers. While they do this, collect the pictures.
5 Ask the class to come and sit very close together in front of you.
6 Hold up Group A's picture for about one minute, moving it steadily around so that everyone gets a good look. Then conceal the card.
7 Group A then take it in turns to ask their ten questions to the other groups, who shout out the answers. If the other groups get an answer right, then there are no points; if they get it wrong it is a point to Group A. You act as umpire, and ask for a show of hands on disputed answers.
8 This continues until all the groups have asked their questions, and then the group with the most points is declared winner.

NOTES

a This activity is called 'Kim's cards' because it is based on 'Kim's game' (from the novel *Kim* by Rudyard Kipling) in which people are shown a number of objects for a limited time and then have to write down what they saw.
b Stage 3 is important if the 'game' part of the activity is going to work well. You need to consult with each group individually over what are 'suitable' questions. Another possibility is that you play the game against the whole class first, thereby modelling it, so the learners see for themselves what is appropriate or not.
c It is important that you keep the momentum going in the last part of the game, and are firm over what is right and wrong.
d This activity was first presented in my article 'Variations on Kim's Game' (Hill 1985).

2.1

LEVEL
Lower intermediate +

TIME
30–45 minutes

FOCUS
Asking *Wh* questions

VISUALS
Enough 20 × 30 cm pictures for one between five or six; preferably colour, showing scenes with a lot going on, people doing different things and a lot of clearly visible objects

2.2

LEVEL
Intermediate +

TIME
20 minutes

FOCUS
Giving reasons;
justifying;
disagreeing

VISUALS
Enough packs of
dominoes cards for
one between four;
packs consist of
twenty-eight 10 × 4
cm cards with a
different picture at
each end. No picture
in the pack should be
of the same thing

PICTURE DOMINOES

Procedure

1 Divide the class into groups of four, and give each group a pack of domino cards. Ask one learner in each group to be the dealer.

2 The dealer gives seven cards to each player. The players look carefully at their cards, and may ask you about anything they are not sure of.

3 The person on the dealer's left begins by putting down a card. The next person then puts a card at either one end or the other of the card on the table, and gives a reason for doing so (e.g. *they are both things to eat; this butterfly likes those flowers*). If the other three players think the reason is good, the card stays; if two of them at least think it is not a good reason the player must pick the card up. In either case the turn passes to the next person on the left.

4 The game proceeds until somebody has got rid of all seven cards, and is declared winner. The others may then continue, to use up their remaining cards.

NOTES

a It is important to stress that the learners should give a full justification of their juxtaposition of two cards.

b Equally, you must stress that the other three players should discuss juxtapositions which they do not agree with; they must not just accept things.

c As the game progresses, and the choice of cards becomes more limited, the juxtapositions become more tenuous. This is where a little imagination is needed, and you might give some assistance on occasions.

d This game was originally described in Byrne and Rixon (1979, p. 40.)

VARIATIONS

1 For lower level learners, cards can be made within a certain lexical field. For example, on one end of each card stick a picture of a piece of furniture or a household utensil, and on the other end stick a 'space' (room, garden, garage, etc.). The game continues as described above, within the boundary of a particular set of language which you wish to practise. There is less room, however, for discussion about juxtapositions, which will largely be obviously right or wrong.

2 To open up the activity to more personal feelings, at one end of the card stick pictures of a very wide range of people (old, young, poor, rich, different cultures, etc.) and on the other end stick pictures of an equally wide range of places (town, country, pretty, ugly, etc.) The game is then to justify why a particular person has been put next to a certain place. There is far more personal reasoning in this version. This activity is best done with more advanced learners.

PELMANISM

Procedure

1 Divide the class into groups of four, with a pack of cards for each group.
2 Ask the learners to lay the cards face down on the desk in six rows of five cards.
3 The first learner turns any two cards face up on the desk, and tries to make a reason for connecting them. If two of the other three players agree that the reason is valid, then that player may pick up the cards. If two out of three disagree the cards are turned back over. In both cases the turn passes to the next player.
4 This continues until all the cards have been picked up, and the winner is the person with the most cards.

NOTES

a It is vital to make your own sets of cards for this game as the commercially available sets have two of each picture, making it solely a memory game and cutting out the need for any of the language of justification and disagreement.
b It is important to tell learners to try and remember the position of cards which have been turned back over, as this will help them to know where there is something which will go with a new card very nicely.
c You should stress that cards must not be picked up when turned over: in this way the others can see the pictures, for discussion. It also makes it easier to remember where they are for future use.
d I first saw this idea written up by Horner (1984). Pelmanism also goes by the name concentration.

VARIATIONS

The language may be controlled very easily by selecting particular pictures for the cards. They could be pictures solely concerned with things and places in the house, with food and drink, and so on.

2.3

LEVEL
Intermediate +

TIME
20 minutes

FOCUS
Giving reasons; justifying; disagreeing

VISUALS
One pack of thirty cards (10 × 7 cm is a good size) for each group with a different picture on each card

2.4

LEVEL
Intermediate +

TIME
30 minutes

FOCUS
Describing and
negotiating
(bargaining)

VISUALS
Sets of sixteen cards
as follows:
1 take four pictures
of similar subject
and size
2 cut each picture
into four parts and
stick them onto
similar-sized
pieces of card so
that when the
correct four cards
are together, a
complete picture
is formed

NEGOTIATION

Procedure

1 Divide the class into groups of four or five and give each group randomly four of the pictures. They look at them and try to put them together, to see if any already match, and which ones they need to exchange.

2 Two of the group stay seated at the table whilst the other two/three go off to negotiate with other groups for the pieces they need to complete their picture. All the cards must be left 'at home', so that the 'travelling salesmen' must describe the pieces they need, and those they wish to swap. A deal is worked out and the pieces are traded.

3 This continues until one group has a complete picture, and so wins. The other groups then take the pieces to complete their pictures.

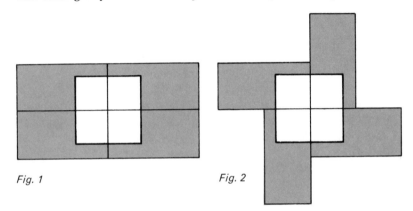

Fig. 1   *Fig. 2*

NOTES

a Try varying the cards from a standard (Fig. 1) to a non-standard (Fig. 2) format. This makes the 'piecing-together' part of the activity more of a puzzle, and consequently there is more to talk about.

b Once the negotiation activity starts, this is a very dynamic activity, with people dashing from table to table clinching deals, breaking them, swapping pictures and celebrating a correct part gained. You are freed to stand back and concentrate on the language being used for later feedback purposes. You should let the activity move at its own pace, and only intervene when really necessary.

c I first learnt this activity when working on the British Council Summer School at Exeter University in 1984.

VARIATIONS

1 Try using four unrelated pictures (e.g. a landscape, a room, a car, a horse)

2 I have also done this activity using sets of four picture stories. Ideal (if rather large) are the *Picture Pack* materials (McGrath 1981).

WHAT AM I?

Procedure

1 Ask the learners to stand around in a circle, all facing inwards.
2 Clip a picture to the back of each learner (they should not see the picture). They must not tell each other what they have on their backs (i.e. what object they are).
3 They must circulate, mix and ask each other questions which can only be answered by *Yes* and *No,* until they discover what object they are.
4 After they have discovered what they are, they should keep circulating, answering questions, and helping other learners find out their own objects.

NOTES

The activity can be done with any recently-learnt set of vocabulary for practice: food, clothes, etc.

VARIATIONS

1 You can make the activity more difficult by making a rule that learners may only ask one question of each person in the group (it's a good idea for them to have a class list and tick off those whom they have asked). With small groups the questions have to be very pertinent.
2 At the end of the activity, the learners can discuss the appropriateness of the object that they 'are' to their character. They can then choose another object (from the same lexical area) which they feel is more suitable for them, and/or give their original object to a person in the group whom they feel it suits better, giving reasons for the decisions in both cases.

2.5

LEVEL
Lower intermediate +

TIME
15 minutes

FOCUS
Asking *Yes/No* questions

VISUALS
Small (maximum 8 × 8 cm) pictures of household objects (utensils, furniture, etc.); one for each learner

OTHER MATERIALS
Conference tags, pins, etc. to attach the pictures

2.6

LEVEL

Lower
intermediate +

TIME

30 minutes

FOCUS

Giving reasons;
discussion; sentence
construction

VISUALS

Four sets of small (5
× 5 cm) cards per
group, consisting of
twenty cards each of
people (who),
objects (what),
places (where) and
people (to whom)

WHO'S TAKING WHAT WHERE AND TO WHOM?

Procedure

1 Ask the learners to get into groups of four, and give a set of cards to each group.

2 Place the cards face down in four piles. Learner A turns over the top card of each pile (a boy, a spanner, a church, a woman, etc.) and then has to link the four pictures by a reason. For example, *the boy is taking the spanner to church to his mother – she telephoned to say her car had broken down.*

3 If two of the other three in the group agree that the sentence (language) and the reason (logic) are good, Learner A keeps the four cards. If they disagree, the turn passes to Learner B, and so on until someone makes an acceptable sentence. If no one does so, the cards are removed. In all these cases, the turn then passes to the next player.

4 The game continues until all the cards have been used up from the central piles; the player with the most cards is the winner.

NOTES

There should usually be a good range of objects, places and people on the cards in order to give the learners' imaginations full scope, to stimulate them to use a wide range of language and to maintain interest.

VARIATIONS

1 You can keep the language level lower and more tightly focused by limiting the range of pictures in one of the sets (e.g. limit the objects solely to household utensils, and the places to rooms).

2 There are numerous possible variations based on this format (e.g. person/place/person: who met whom where; person/vehicle/place: who went where how, etc.). Byrne (1978) has described some such activities in his instruction booklet.

I'M WITH YOU

Procedure

2.7

LEVEL
Beginner – lower
intermediate

TIME
20 minutes

FOCUS
Vocabulary
associations and
giving reasons

VISUALS
A set of pictures
showing household
'spaces' (rooms,
garden, garage, etc.)
and the things which
go in them (furniture
and fittings); one for
each learner

1 Give each learner a picture. Tell them not to show it to anyone else. Most of them should have pictures of furniture and fittings, but a few (say eight in a class of thirty) should have 'spaces'.
2 Tell the learners that those with furniture and fittings must go and find the right space to be with, and vice versa. They should do this by asking questions; not by showing pictures.
3 As soon as there are more than two people around each 'space', the acceptance of other people into that 'space' must depend on group discussion. Rejected furniture and fittings must try elsewhere.
4 When everyone is with a group, the groups take it in turns to explain what 'space' they are, and what is in that 'space'. The other groups agree and disagree. If there is a majority decision that someone is with the wrong group, they must move elsewhere.

NOTES

This activity is more fun with a large class, where there might be six or eight 'spaces' and twenty-four people with furniture and fittings. With smaller groups it becomes a quieter and more considered activity, where choices are discussed in greater depth. In this situation it is a good idea to include a high number of kinds of furniture and fittings which will go in more than one space.

VARIATIONS

This format works very well with many different areas of vocabulary. It can be done with occupations and clothes, meals and food, animals and habitats, and so on.

CHAPTER 3

Structures

3.1

LEVEL
Intermediate +

TIME
5–15 minutes

FOCUS
Asking *Yes/No*
questions

VISUALS
A single picture
which will provoke a
real response when
seen (of amusement,
surprise, disgust,
etc.); it should be
large (20 × 30 cm),
and should
incorporate known
things in unusual
juxtaposition

NOSEY PARKER

Procedure

1 Let the class see that you have a picture, but keep it hidden. Tell the learners that they must find out what is in the picture by asking questions to which you are able to answer *Yes* or *No*.

2 The learners ask questions until they discover what is in the picture; they are then shown it.

NOTES

a The success of this activity depends firstly on the picture having sufficient intrinsic interest to stimulate genuine questioning. (You will find that if a good picture is used the first time, the questioning will be far more enthusiastic next time.) I have pictures of five pigs in a filthy washroom, an open mouth with a fly on a fork, an old man playing dominoes with a dog, a girl waterskiing behind Nessie, and so on.

b Success also depends on the sensitivity with which you answer the questions. Besides *Yes* and *No,* a range of clue answers can be given: *I can't see, I don't know* (i.e. it's not visible), *It's not important,* and answers emphasising parts of the question which are incorrect (*'Is there a man?' 'Not a man . . .' 'Oh . . . Are there some men?' 'Yes'*). It is also useful to suggest that learners proceed from the general to the specific, e.g. if they are given an affirmative answer to the question *Is there an animal in the picture?,* and then shout out the names of single animals it could take hours to reach the right one. They should be encouraged to ask (in this case) if the animals are domestic or wild, whether they eat meat or grass (or if they are herbivores or carnivores, with an advanced class), so narrowing the choice down before asking specific questions.

VARIATIONS

The activity works just as well with a pair (or pair of pairs) asking each other. The only constraint is whether you have enough of the right kind of pictures.

ACKNOWLEDGEMENT
I learnt this technique from Harley Brookes (then ELO, British Council, Milan) during a seminar at Centro di Lingue Moderne Trento in 1978.

WHAT WOULD YOU DO?

3.2

Procedure

1 Ask the class to get into pairs (or groups of three or four depending on how many pictures you have). Give each pair (group) a pile of about twenty pictures each, face down.
2 Learner A turns over the top card, and asks Learner B an appropriate question e.g. *What would you do if you were on the balcony of a burning building?*
3 Learner B makes an appropriate reply.
4 If the other(s) agree that this is a good answer, Learner B keeps the card; if not it is put at the bottom of the pile.
5 The learners take it in turns to ask each other questions until all of the cards have been taken.

NOTES

You should decide beforehand how full you want the answer at Stage 3 to be: do you want *If I were on the balcony of a burning building, I'd . . .* or is *I'd . . .* enough?

LEVEL
Intermediate +

TIME
30 minutes

FOCUS
Second conditional

VISUALS
One set of about twenty pictures for each group, showing people in difficult situations (e.g. on the balcony of a blazing building; stepping out of a plane surrounded by masked gunmen; up a tree with a large dog barking below, etc.)

3.3

LEVEL
Lower intermediate

TIME
15 minutes

FOCUS
Past simple

VISUALS
One set of about twenty (12 × 8 cm) cards for each group, showing single actions

WHEN DID YOU LAST . . . ?

Procedure

1 Divide the class into groups of four. Give each group a set of about twenty cards, face down in a pile.

2 Learner A turns over the top card, and asks Learner B *When did you last . . . ?*, putting the verb indicated by the action in the picture into the question. Learner B answers truthfully.

3 Learner C then asks Learner B any other question about the answer given, to which Learner B must reply, again truthfully:

A: (turns over picture of someone writing a letter) When did you last write a letter?
B: On Sunday.
C: Who did you write to?
B: My mother.

4 When the interaction finishes, Learner D turns over the next card and asks Learner A. The activity continues until all the cards have been used up.

NOTES

a As this activity requires truthfulness in the answers, it is a good idea to pre-teach *I have never done that* in case the situation arises. The learners are unlikely to have learnt the present perfect before the past simple and it saves difficulties with the past participles of irregular verbs, and prevents the incorrect use of the past simple.

b If desired, this activity can go on much longer by going through the same cards again with different members of the group asking and answering the questions.

VARIATIONS

This activity works almost as well with the future – *When will you next . . . ?* – although learners need to be taught how to use *probably* and *possibly*:

A: (turns over card showing someone drinking coffee) When will you next drink a cup of coffee?
B: After the lesson.
C: Where will you drink it?
B: I'll probably drink it in the bar next to my house.

NATIONALITIES AND COUNTRIES OF ORIGIN

Procedure

1 Turn over the top picture from the pile of portraits and ask *Who's this?* The learners reply.
2 Then ask *Where's* (Margaret Thatcher) *from?* and wait for a reply.
3 Carry on with another picture, as in Stage 1, but when you get to the second question ask *What nationality is* (Robert Redford)?
4 Carry on in this way, alternating the second question.

VARIATIONS

This can be done as a group activity, as follows:
1 Ask the learners to get into groups; give each group a set of about twenty small (10 × 8 cm) pictures of famous people.
2 The interaction should go as follows:

    A: (turns over top card) Who's this?
    B: (answers, if possible) It's Michael Jackson.
    A: Where's he from?
    C: (answers, if possible) He's from America.
    A: What nationality is he?
    D: (answers, if possible) He's American.

3 The learners take it in turns to ask the questions, until all the cards have been used up.
4 The activity can be made into a game, with points:
One point for a correct answer; half a point for answering a question answered incorrectly by another learner; half a point for answering a question another learner cannot answer.

3.4

LEVEL
Beginner –
intermediate

TIME
15 minutes

FOCUS
Names of
nationalities and
countries

VISUALS
A set of portraits of
internationally
famous people from
different walks of life
(sport, politics,
cinema, music, etc.)
from all over the
world

3.5

TELL ME WHAT I DID

LEVEL
Lower
intermediate +

TIME
20 minutes

FOCUS
Narrating past
events; asking
questions about past
events

VISUALS
A large number of
small (5 × 5 cm)
pictures illustrating
actions for each pair

Procedure

1 Ask the learners to pair off. Give each pair a large number of action pictures.
2 Ask the class to think about how they spent their last non-school day/ free day.
3 Ask the Learner A's in each pair to select from the pile as many pictures as they can find which illustrate their day. They should lay these pictures on the desk in order, leaving gaps in the sequence for any major events for which they have no picture. If there are pictures for all the activities done by Learner A, one or two can be left out.
4 When the sequence is ready, the Learner Bs then tell the Learner As what they did. Every time there is a gap, they should either make a suggestion (*Did you eat your dinner next?*) or ask a direct question (*What did you do next?*).
5 When Learner B has discovered the sequence, the activity should be repeated the other way round.
6 Finally, the learners can write up the other person's day from memory.

NOTES

a The set of cards needs to be quite large, with repeats of some actions (e.g. eating) which will have occurred more than once. The typical sequence should be about ten–fifteen pictures long.
b If you have enough pictures (or a small group), both learners in the pair should prepare their sequences simultaneously.
c If there are not enough cards, ask Learner B to write down the day's activities in note form while Learner A lays down the sequence. Learner A must not see the notes.
d This is a useful activity for practising sequencers (*first, then, next, after that, etc.*).

VARIATIONS

This format works well for 'intermediate +' learners as a practice for *What I'd like to do on a particular day, if this were the best of all possible worlds*.

OCCUPATION vs ACTION

Procedure

1 Provide a pile of pictures as described. Hold them up and ask *What does s/he do?*
2 If and when the correct answer is given, then ask *What is s/he doing?*
3 If and when the correct answer is given, take another pictuure and repeat the process.

NOTES

This activity is plainly only useful at the point in a course where these two items have been learnt and are in danger of being (or are being) confused. It can also be used for revision.

VARIATIONS

Given enough pictures of this type (and they are not very easy to find!), this activity could be turned into a learner-learner activity, in pairs or groups.

3.6

LEVEL
Beginner

TIME
15 minutes

FOCUS
Use of *What does s/he do?* and *What's s/he doing?*

VISUALS
Pictures of people who obviously (by their dress) do a particular job but who are performing another action (e.g. a judge in wig and gown eating a meal; a chef in hat and apron reading a newspaper)

CHAPTER 4

Fluency

4.1

LEVEL
Intermediate +

TIME
20 minutes

FOCUS
Describing and giving
reasons

VISUALS
Pictures of roads in
different out-of-town
situations (running
through forests, over
hills, by lakes, etc.):
at least one for each
learner

ROADS

Procedure

1 Give the learners the chance to choose the picture which they want, either by selecting from pictures scattered around the room, or from piles given to each group.

2 Then ask the learners to do some or all of the following activities:

   a Explain to a partner why they chose that particular picture. Encourage the learners to talk about the memories and associations which the picture they have chosen evokes.

   b Describe it (orally or in writing).

   c Decide on, describe and explain (orally or in writing) what lies at the end of the road, beyond where it finishes in the picture, and/or where the road comes from.

   d A timed whole-class exercise: tell the learners they have one minute to note down each of the following:

   i two things they can see to the left as they walk down the road;

   ii two things they can hear as they walk down the road;

   iii two things they can see to the right as they walk down the road;

   iv two things they can smell as they walk down the road;

   v two things they pick up as they walk down the road;

   vi something they can see which they don't like as they walk down the road.

   They then share their lists with other members of the class, whilst looking at the picture. (If you have double copies of the same pictures, it is interesting to give them, unseen, around the class, and ask the learners to find the person with the same picture and discuss similarities and differences.)

   e Ask the learners to circulate, look at each others' pictures, and find a road (some roads) which has (have) a junction with their road at some point. When pairs/groups have formed, they should get together with other pairs/groups and explain their reasons.

ACKNOWLEDGEMENT
The activities presented here have their roots in a seed planted by Branka Aleksic-Hill.

FEET

Procedure

1 Check that the class know all the basic vocabulary associated with feet (*big toe, ankle, instep, etc.*)
2 Ask the learners to get into pairs/groups. Give each individual a picture of someone's feet, and ask them – alone – to decide to whom they belong (What sort of person? Why?).
3 They should then explain their ideas to their partner/group, who should agree or disagree.
4 Tell the pairs/groups that the owners of their feet are connected in some way they should then decide upon the relationship between them.
5 They should then explain this relationship to other pairs/groups for comment.

NOTES

It is important that the learners do not see each other's pictures until Stage 3; they may be influenced by those ideas, which will lessen the value of Stage 4. Not knowing what they are going to do in Stage 4 will go some way to preventing this.

VARIATIONS

1 Give the learners only pictures of bare feet, and at the end of the activity as described above, they select appropriate footware for their feet from a large pile of pictures, showing everything from Wellington boots to ballet shoes, from mountaineering boots to sandals; female and male; old and new; cheap and expensive; clean and dirty. They discuss their choice with the other learners.
2 At the end of the activity, the learners match their feet (shod and/or bare) to an appropriate face from piles at their disposal. They discuss their choice with other learners.
3 At the end of the activity, the learners match their feet with pictures of hands of all types at their disposal. (It is interesting to match bare feet/bare hands and shod feet/gloved hands, as well as the contrary.)

ACKNOWLEDGEMENT
Branka Aleksic-Hill first suggested the idea of working with 'feet' pictures to me.

4.2

LEVEL
Intermediate +

TIME
20 minutes

FOCUS
Giving reasons and justifying

VISUALS
Pictures (medium – large size) of feet of all types – shod and bare; one for each learner

4.3

LEVEL
Intermediate +

TIME
30 minutes

FOCUS
Giving reasons and
justifying

VISUALS
Envelopes (one per
group) with pictures
of six to ten things
which were found in
the possession of a
criminal. They
should be a mixture
of usual things, plus
one or two 'criminal'
items. Pictures of a
letter, tickets and a
passport are useful

**OTHER
MATERIALS**
Typed warrants for
arrest, giving details
of the crime

THE CASE FOR THE ARREST

Procedure

1 Give the learners – in groups of three or four – an envelope of pictures
and an arrest warrant.
2 Tell them that they have just arrested the person in question, and that
the objects in the pictures were found in the possession of that
person.
3 The learners should read the warrant and try to show how the objects
relate to the crime that has been committed, and decide why the
person is guilty.
4 After the groups have worked out their cases, they should get
together in pairs of groups. Each group presents its case, while the
other group acts as the defence, trying to point out weaknesses in the
case. The 'prosecutors' should argue back and try to convince them.

NOTES

a Prepare the arrest warrants to go with particular sets of pictures in
order to get a good match between objects and people arrested.
b The warrant could resemble the illustration. The envelope, marked
'HILL'S POSSESSIONS', could contain pictures of London theatre
tickets, a pipe, a penknife, a letter (to Holmes), and so on.

WARRANT FOR THE ARREST
of

......**David A. Hill**......

wanted for questioning in connection with the murder of
Richard John Holmes on 12th November 1989 at his flat at
15 Victoria Drive, Leeds. Holmes was stabbed with a knife.

Evidence against Hill: a tin of pipe tobacco found in Holmes'
flat; Hill is known to have gone to the theatre on
11th November; Hill is known to have been a friend of Holmes'

VARIATIONS

You can give the learners piles of pictures and ask them to work out a
crime, write the arrest warrant and select suitable pictures to go with it.
They can then give this to another pair/group to work out.

WHAT DID I CUT OUT?

Procedure

1 Give each learner a picture, which must not be seen by the other learners.
2 Ask the learners to study their pictures secretly; they must decide what is the most and what is the least important 'thing' (object, person, action) in the picture in relation to the main action/interaction.
3 Next the learners should cut out these two details from the picture (as a generally oval/circular/rectangular shape, rather than the shape itself), being careful not to damage the rest of the picture. They should hide the two shapes from the other.
4 Ask the learners to get into pairs; they should take it in turns to show their pictures, while the other decides what is missing and why. *Yes/No* questions may be asked.
5 Once a learner has discovered what is missing, the parts can be put back.

VARIATIONS

1 The learners can show each other the parts they cut out, and hide the whole picture; the object is then to describe the whole.
2 After doing the activity once, the learners can change partners and do it again.

4.4

LEVEL
Lower intermediate +

TIME
20 minutes

FOCUS
Giving reasons and justifying

VISUALS
An unmounted picture for each learner. The pictures must be of an event, with an interaction or action in the foreground, but with a lot of other detail around it

OTHER MATERIALS
Pairs of small pointed scissors (nail scissors)

4.5

LEVEL
Intermediate +

TIME
20 minutes

FOCUS
Giving reasons and justifying

VISUALS
Enough half-pictures for the class to have two halves each; the half-pictures are made by taking twice as many pictures (no smaller than 15 × 15 cm) as there are learners in the class, and cutting them in half in exactly the same way. You should keep half the part B's and half the part A's (non-matching) and discard the rest (or see Variations)

UNLIKELY MIXTURE

Procedure

1 Give all the learners a part B half of a picture. Scatter the non-matching part A halves around the classroom.

2 Ask the learners to think carefully what the missing halves to their pictures are like; this should be in terms of colour, shapes and textures, as well as objects, people and features.

3 Then the learners should circulate, looking at the part A halves around the room, and trying to decide which one would best complete their picture.

4 They should then sit next to it. If they are the only person wanting a particular picture, they can take it and form a group with three or four others. If two or more people want the same picture, they should sit together with it.

5 Individuals should then tell each other why they wanted that particular piece to complete their picture. The others should listen and comment on their choice.

NOTES

a It may seem logical to aid better matching by giving out pictures with only one image type (e.g. all colour photos); I have found, however, that a variety of image types is often more helpful for learners, and certainly provokes far more discussion at Stage 5.

b Except with very small groups – ten and under – it is unnecessary to add extra half-pictures to those scattered around the room; the small choice forces learners to look at their pictures even more closely in order to find a piece which will best complete their picture.

VARIATIONS

After Stage 5, you may like to give learners the real piece which completes their picture; this can then be compared with the piece they chose to best complete it.

PEOPLE AND PLACES

Procedure

1 Each learner selects a portrait picture without showing it to anyone else.
2 Ask the learners to take time thinking about their person in terms of their physical appearance and the type of person they are: character, life-style, habits, and so on. While they do this, you should put the place pictures up around the classroom.
3 Then ask the learners to get up and walk around the room, look at the place pictures and try to decide which place would be most suitable for their person: they should work out reasons why.
4 Finally, ask them to take the pictures of places with them, choose a partner, and explain why they have chosen that picture. They should also listen to and discuss their partner's choice.

NOTES

a It is important to give the learners enough time to build up the character of the person before they go off to select a place picture. You could include some writing at this stage – a written physical and character description – in order to focus the learners' attention.
b At Stage 3, it may well happen that two or more learners want the same place picture for their person, if so, they should sit together for Stage 4.

VARIATIONS

1 After Stage 4 the learners can move on to find another partner with whom to discuss connections.
2 You may wish to have a written outcome for this exercise. A good follow-up is to ask the learners to write one side of A4 (only) about the person, the place and the connection, then leave it next to the two pictures on their desk. The whole class then circulates, reading and commenting (either verbally to each other, or by writing a sentence on the paper).
3 Variation 2 of 'Picture dominoes' (p. 22) formalises this idea into a game.
4 This activity works just as well if the pictures on the wall are of 'personal' objects: possessions such as clothes, cars, houses, electrical equipment, and/or more personal things such as pens, books, cigarette lighters, and so on.

4.6

LEVEL
Intermediate +

TIME
30 minutes

FOCUS
Describing the character of people and places; giving reasons and justifying

VISUALS
Enough portrait pictures of unknown people for everyone in the class to have one; the same number (or preferably more) pictures of places. The range of both types of picture should be as wide as possible

4.7

TIME
30 minutes

FOCUS
Classifying and
justifying names of
animals

VISUALS
Enough sets of
pictures of thirty
different animals (5
× 5 cm) for groups of
four to have one set
each. (The sets
should be identical.)

CLASSIFICATION

Procedure

1 Divide the class into groups of four, and give each group a set of pictures.
2 Ask the groups to work together to classify the animals in any way they like. (I usually explain that they could leave them all together as one group and call them 'animals', or separate them into thirty single pictures and call each set of one picture by the name of the animal species, but that I want something in between.)
3 You should circulate, helping with names and categories if asked.
4 Elicit the categories used for classification by the groups and list them on the board in columns based on the nature of the category (e.g columns of habitats; of food; ways of moving; etc.)
5 Put up the classification categories in columns and then ask the learners for the reasons for their connection, and a title for each column.
6 Next, ask the groups to reclassify their pictures, using any other categories they can think of except those on the board.
7 Then elicit the new categories and add them to the list.

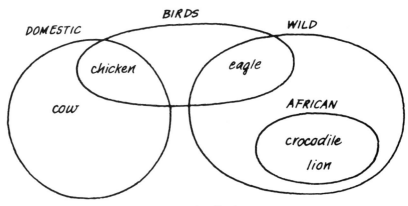

Fig. 3 An example of the use of sets in classification

NOTES

a This is good for vocabulary expansion, not only with the names of animals, but also the categories, e.g. at lower levels 'animals which eat grass' may be fine, but later on they should know 'herbivores'.
b I have found the mathematical concept of 'setting' a useful one in dividing up the different categories, for in that way one animal can be in two or more groups at the same time.
c I first presented this idea at TESOL in Rome, in November 1987.

VARIATIONS

This activity works well with any area of language which is cross-classifiable; food, clothes and transport are three obvious areas.

ODD MAN OUT

4.8

LEVEL
Intermediate +

TIME
20 minutes

FOCUS
Group discussion,
giving reasons and
justifying

VISUALS
A random selection
of pictures, but all of
the same image type
(i.e. all colour
drawings, all black
and white
photographs); one
for each learner

Procedure

1 Divide the class into groups of eight to ten, and give each member of the group a picture.
2 Ask the groups to look at each other's pictures and talk about them; tell them that they must come to a decision about which is the 'odd man out'. It is important to stress that those in danger of being nominated 'odd man out' should argue why they should stay in the group.
3 The groups then report their decision to the other groups, who should comment upon it.

NOTES

a It is important that the image type of the pictures is the same, otherwise that might be taken as the reason for the exclusion, which would not be very generative of language.
b In my experience, eight to ten is the ideal number for a group for this activity; smaller groups don't have enough to talk about, and larger groups allow too many learners to be not very involved.

VARIATIONS

1 Instead of arguing why they should not be excluded, the object of the activity can be changed, so that the winner is the person who is excluded. The learners should argue with reasons about why their picture has less than the others to do with the majority of the pictures.
2 You can put sets of pictures on the wall (as many sets as there are groups in the class); the learners circulate as a group, with equal time (say five minutes) in front of each set of pictures. They should agree why a particular picture is the 'odd man out'. They move from set to set, and eventually, as a class, compare and discuss ideas. You may wish to keep notes on the board.

4.9

LEVEL
Intermediate +

TIME
30 minutes

FOCUS
Describing and
justifying

VISUALS
A set of pictures
looking through
windows from the
inside to the outside;
at least one for each
learner

LOOK THROUGH ANY WINDOW

Procedure

1 Ask the learners to select a picture each and to get into pairs.
2 They must come to a decision about exactly what they can see through their windows, and also what sort of place they are in.
3 This done, ask the pairs to join into groups of four, and explain their ideas to each other; they should ask each other for reasons for their decisions.

NOTES

a It is important that the pictures used do not show too much of the room (or 'area') in front of and around the window, but should be cut or masked so that just the frame and wall immediately next to it are visible, along with the view outside the window. This allows for more invention, speculation and discussion in Stage 3.
b Maley *et al*(1980, pp. 89–90) works with windows.

VARIATIONS

1 This can be turned into a matching activity, either as a follow-up to the activity described above, or as a separate activity:
  a The learners look through a resource bank of pictures of people and choose the one who habitually looks through the window they have chosen.
  b The learners look through a resource bank of pictures of buildings, seen entire and from the outside, and decide which one their window belongs to.
  In both cases, the learners have to justify their choices to each other.

ACKNOWLEDGEMENT
The activity is based on an idea by Branka Aleksic-Hill.

COLOUR MY PICTURE

Procedure

1 Elicit from the learners what associations they have with particular colours; list their ideas on the board.
2 Ask the learners to get into groups of five to seven and give them each a picture. They should not talk about the pictures at this stage.
3 Each learner should write down a colour which to them sums up the mood of the picture; they must not show this to anyone else.
4 The pictures are passed on to the next person, and a colour is noted and so on, until all the pictures have been seen by each member of the group, and they have the picture they started with.
5 The pictures should be spread out so they can all be seen, and the group should break into subgroups of two or three to discuuss their ideas.
6 After a while, different subgroups can be formed, and the discussion continued.

NOTES

a This is a good activity for introducing or revising the use of colours, nuances (**greyish**-*blue,* **reddish**-*brown*), intensifiers (**pale** *green,* **dark** *red)* and modifying adjectives (**dove** *grey,* **charcoal** *grey*).
b It is very important that the individual colour ideas for each picture chosen (at Stages 3 and 4) are kept completely secret until all of the group have seen all of the pictures, otherwise there is the risk of ideas being spread; if this happens it lessens the interest in the discussion which follows.

VARIATIONS

At the end of the discussion section, the whole group can sum up its reactions to the pictures in a series of written sentences which use the language of comparison and contrast, e.g. *Whereas most of the group thought this picture was green, two people thought it was yellow; this was because* .... These sentences can be left next to the pictures, and the groups can walk around and see what the others have produced.

4.10

LEVEL
Intermediate +

TIME
30 minutes

FOCUS
Expressing personal feelings, justifying

VISUALS
A set of moody 'emotional' black and white photos; one for each

4.11

LEVEL
Lower
intermediate +

TIME
15 minutes

FOCUS
Group dynamics;
discussing character

VISUALS
Pictures of many
different sorts of cars
(saloons/sports,
expensive/cheap, old/
new, fast/slow, etc.);
a number of pictures
for each learner

YOU'RE A VOLVO!

Procedure

1 Give each learner a number of pictures of cars and ask them to think about them and decide what kind of car they are, in terms of appearance and character.

2 Ask them to try and find a similarity between one of the cars and someone in the group; they should think carefully about their reasons.

3 The group should then get up and tell everyone else in the group about their ideas except the person they have matched the car with; the listeners should comment on the match and say whether they agree or disagree, and why.

4 Finally, each learner should put their idea to the person, including, the suggestions from the rest of the group; they should see what the person feels about the match.

NOTES

a This activity relies upon the group knowing something about each other, and should be done after at least twenty-five hours of group work together.

b In choosing the pictures, it is important to have a very broad range of types and styles of cars, as many people do not know about the generally accepted character of a car just from the name.

VARIATIONS

1 There may be a final group discussion where all these ideas are presented. (For large classes, it is a good idea to do the whole exercise in groups of not more than fifteen.)

2 After, or instead of, the group discussion, all the car pictures may be laid on the table and the learners go and select
   a a better picture for the same person
   b a suitable picture for someone else which has not been mentioned before.

DESERT ISLANDS

Procedure

1 Ask the class to get into groups of four to six. Give each group one of the identical sets of pictures of objects.
2 Ask the learners to spread the pictures out, look at them and talk about them.
3 Tell them that they have been shipwrecked, and these are the things which are left; ask them to choose (mentally) which two objects they would take with them and think of reasons why.
4 Then ask the learners to tell each other what they took and why; the others in the group should comment on the choice and reasons. The group can make a list of what, communally, they have brought with them.
5 Next, give each group a question mark, and tell them that they should come to a group decision about one other thing they would like to take ashore with them (nothing to help them escape, or contact people directly).
6 The groups compare notes, either
  a as an open whole-class situation, or
  b by getting the Learner A's from each group together, the Learner B's from each group, and so on.

NOTES

a There should be about fifteen objects in each set.
b This activity is based on an idea by Byrne and Wright (1974, p. 60).

VARIATIONS

The activity can be done as a group decision-making exercise, with all the members deciding which objects (eight, for a four-person group) they would take, and what the question mark object should be.

4.12

LEVEL
Intermediate +

TIME
30 minutes

FOCUS
Giving reasons and justifying

VISUALS
Sets of pictures of objects which would be useful/useless on a desert island (knife, axe, gun, chair, guitar, cigarette lighter, books, camera, transistor radio, mirror, money, binoculars, boots, ball, etc.); one set for each group

OTHER MATERIALS
A card with a question mark on it for each set

CHAPTER 5

Writing

5.1

LEVEL
Intermediate +

TIME
30–60 minutes

FOCUS
Personal writing for a
real audience;
discussion

VISUALS
A large selection of
mounted pictures
(ten for every learner
in the class is a good
ratio) with images of
as wide a variety as
possible – the
moodier the better

**OTHER
MATERIALS**
Half-sheets of plain
A4 paper; Blu-tac or
similar adhesive

READING THEIR OWN WRITING

Procedure

1 Ideally, the tables should be arranged in the centre of the room and the chairs put around the edge of the room, facing the walls. The pictures should then be spread, face upwards, on the tables.

2 Ask the learners to walk around the tables, sifting through the pictures, looking at them and talking about them. They should pick up pictures which evoke a strong memory for them, and may hold up to three pictures in their hands at any one time; finally they must keep only one picture.

3 When they have made their final choice, they should take it away, preferably without discussing it with anyone. They should take half a piece of A4 paper, go to a chair and sit facing the wall.

4 They then write about the memory evoked by the picture, on one side of the paper only. Stress that the learners write about the *memory* evoked by the picture and not simply describe it in physical terms.

5 When it is obvious to you that the first learners are finishing, start to collect in the pictures from all the learners. Blu-tac these around the classroom walls.

6 When everyone has finished, the (unsigned) papers are collected, and everyone takes one (not their own!).

7 Ask the learners to read the paper they have chosen very carefully before circulating and looking at the pictures on the wall and trying to decide which picture evoked the written memory. When they are reasonably sure, they may take the picture and try to find the author.

8 Discussion should then follow as the learners relate the link between the picture and the written memory.

NOTES

a Often much interesting discussion arises at Stage 7 when two or more learners think that their writing refers to the same picture.

b I first presented this idea at the Lektor's conference in Dubrovnik in December 1983.

VARIATIONS

Besides a memory, this activity works equally well with areas such as 'something I love, hate, fear, have forgotten', etc.

A ROOM OF ONE'S OWN

Procedure

1 The learners choose (or are given) a picture of a room each. They look at it for a time and then write a short description of it, highlighting the character of the room, on the piece of A4 paper.
2 Ask them to tell their partner what sort of person they imagine living in that room and why; this should include both physical and character details.
3 They then look through the library of portraits to find someone who comes as close as possible to the sort of person they imagined.
4 They take the picture back to their place and write a full character description of the person, including details of work, hobbies, etc., underneath the description of the room.
5 Display the two pictures and the writing on the wall and ask the learners to circulate, reading each others' writing, looking at the pictures and commenting on them.

NOTES

a Whilst you only need enough room pictures for everyone in the class to have one each, it is important to have a large collection of portraits for the learners to choose from, so they have high chance of finding a suitable match.
b It is very important to use pictures of real rooms which are lived in rather than the characterless fakes to be found in architectural and 'home' magazines, made to show off furniture and fabrics.

VARIATIONS

1 This activity may be done using pictures of desks, of gardens (or spaces around houses), and so on, with just as much success.
2 You may wish to make Stage 5 into a feedback session where learners comment on how right they felt each others' room-owner matches were.

5.2

LEVEL
Intermediate +

TIME
15–30 minutes

FOCUS
Describing rooms and justifying matching them with people

VISUALS
A selection of pictures of rooms (a very wide range of types and styles is vital) and a selection of portraits (equally wide-ranging)

OTHER MATERIALS
A4 paper, Blu-tac

5.3

LEVEL
Intermediate +

TIME
30–45 minutes

FOCUS
Using the language of advertising

VISUALS
A selection of the visual part of advertisements for a wide range of products; at least one for each pair

OTHER MATERIALS
One example for each pair of complete advertisements for a wide range of products; A4 paper; Blu-tac

WHAT'S MY ADVERTISEMENT?

Procedure

1 Distribute a pile of complete magazine advertisements (pictures and text) to the learners in pairs. Ask them to look at the adverts carefully; tell them to examine particularly closely the language used, its relationship to the picture and the overall layout.

2 Ask for feedback on what they have found out; list commonly found key points on the board. Add any crucial elements of the advertisements which you feel have been overlooked.

3 Give the learners a pile of pictures from magazine advertisements and ask them in pairs to select the one which they like most.

4 Ask the pairs to decide what their picture is advertising, and to produce the wording to go with it on rough paper.

5 Circulate and check language for correctness, and then, when they have finished the rough version, ask the pairs to produce a fair copy with the picture attached.

6 Attach the finished products to the wall, and invite the pairs to circulate and read each others' work.

7 When they have all seen most of the advertisements produced, there can be an open learners' discussion of their relative values, with reasons.

NOTES

a It is important to give the learners advertisement pictures with which they are not familiar, otherwise there will be little creative language production; this is particularly problematic if you teach in Britain where learners may be exposed to the same visuals as those you want to use on TV, in magazines and on hoardings.

b In order to get results, it is important that the learners pick up the key points of advertisement technique; to that end, you yourself should analyse and understand this technique.

NEWS REPORT

Procedure

1 Give out some newspaper reports of different kinds of events (prefer-ably illustrated); ask the learners to examine the language use and layout of the articles.

2 Elicit feedback on what they have noticed, listing any key points on the board and adding anything important which has been overlooked.

3 Ask the learners to get into pairs, and give each pair a pile of photographs from recent newspapers; ask them to choose one of them.

4 They should now write a newspaper report around the picture, adding a headline and caption. You should circulate as they produce a rough version, helping with language (but not ideas unless strictly necessary).

5 When they have finished, give each pair a piece of A4 paper and ask them to write up their report in the form of a newspaper article, attaching the picture.

6 As the articles are finished, they should be displayed on the wall and the learners invited to go round and read each others' work.

7 When they have read most of them, there can be an open discussion on which ones were best, and why.

NOTES

a It is important that the learners are given 'action' pictures from the newspaper – people doing things, accidents, events – rather than portraits or objects; this gives them more to get hold of.

b The pictures do not, of course, have to come from English language newspapers; they can just as easily come from learner mother tongue papers, as long as the captions are removed. Indeed, photographs showing local colour and events may well be more conducive to good learner writing.

c For the activity to be a valuable exercise in the use of newspaper language, it is important that Stages 1 and 2 are done fully, so that the learners understand the key elements of the form. Books such as Baddock (1983), (1984) and Duff and Schindler (1984) are helpful background.

VARIATIONS

The whole activity could be made into the production of a newspaper, with different pairs creating different articles this obviously needs more careful planning.

5.4

LEVEL
Intermediate +

TIME
30 minutes

FOCUS
Using the language of newspaper reporting

VISUALS
A selection of action photographs from recent newspapers; a pile for each pair

OTHER MATERIALS
A selection of recent newspapers (or authentic examples of newspaper extracts from textbooks); A4 paper; Blu-tac

5.5

TIME
20 minutes

FOCUS
Writing comparisons

VISUALS
One pair of similar
faces (not famous
people); for each
learner; large size

COMPARING FACES

Procedure

1 Once the learners have acquired the basic ability to describe the features of the face, that knowledge can be used to practise the language of comparison, in written form.

2 Give out the pairs of portraits to each learner; it is helpful to get the learners to make a chart about their two pictures, like this one.

FEATURE	PERSON A	PERSON B
shape of face		
complexion		

hair: colour
    length
    type		

eyes: colour shape		
eyelashes		
eyebrows		
forehead		
etc.		

3 Based on this chart (and perhaps on a model provided by you) they can construct a comparative/contrastive description of the two portraits, e.g. *Both of these people are old men, but while the one on the left has grey hair, the one on the right has white hair. Neither of them has a beard or moustache, etc . . . .*

4 Finally they can read each others' work and check it against the pictures, commenting on what is good, and what has been omitted or is wrong.

NOTES

a This technique allows the learners to confront new structures (comparing and contrasting language) whilst using familiar vocabulary (unlike most textbooks which expect them to use a new structure with new vocabulary).

b The compare/contrast approach is not only a learning exercise in its own right, but is also a useful way of checking the learners' assimilation of any set of vocabulary.

STORY MAKING

Procedure

1 Ask the learners to get into pairs; give each pair a set of five pictures, which the other learners shouldn't see.
2 The pair decide on a story which links the five random pictures. They should write this down as a rough version.
3 As they work, circulate, helping with language (and ideas if absolutely necessary) and checking the rough versions.
4 When they have finished, they can write up the story as a fair copy.
5 The sets of pictures are now displayed. Give each pair another pair's story to read and ask them to decide which set of pictures illustrates it. They should keep a note of their decision, and exchange stories without saying anything.
6 This continues until they have read (almost) all the stories and decided which sets of pictures go with each of them. There can then be a whole-class pooling of ideas, as each pair explains the ideas for their story.

LEVEL
Intermediate +

TIME
40 minutes

FOCUS
Writing a story for people to read

VISUALS
One set for each learner containing five unrelated pictures of the same image-type (i.e. all drawings; all colour photographs)

NOTES

It is important that the learners keep their pictures and their ideas to themselves, otherwise the point of the climax of the activity is lost.

VARIATIONS

This activity can be done very well by learners telling their stories onto tapes, and the other pairs listening; it then changes, of course, into an oral/aural activity, not writing/reading.

5.7

PICTURE THE SCENE

LEVEL

Intermediate +

TIME

45 minutes

FOCUS

Writing a story for other people to listen to

VISUALS

One set for each learner of three pictures which have a connection in action

Procedure

1 Give every learner a set of three related pictures. Explain that the pictures show three scenes from the same story, and that the learners should write a story which includes them at some point.

2 As they write, circulate, helping with vocabulary as required.

3 When they have all finished, ask them to get into pairs; Learner A should give B the three pictures, and read the story. Learner B should look at the pictures and indicate when the story arrives at the point where that scene occurs. A says whether it is correct or not.

4 They should then do the activity the other way round. After this they can change partners and repeat the activity again.

NOTES

a It is better if the learners keep their story and picture order to themselves until Stage 3 or the activity will lose its point.

b In making the sets of three pictures it is important that the 'feel' of the images is the same, rather than the actions shown are very closely related. For this reason, it is better to keep sets within the same image type (e.g. all colour photographs, all cartoon drawings, etc.).

VARIATIONS

At the end of Stage 3, ask the learners to write down their stories, and leave them with the three pictures. They can then circulate, reading each others' stories and deciding on the order of the three scenes.

CHAPTER 6

Listening

SPOT THE SIMILARITY

Procedure

1 Ask the learners to get into pairs (or pairs of pairs). Give each learner (or pair) a picture which the other(s) must not see.
2 Tell them that they have pictures which are very different from each other, and ask them to describe their pictures to each other with the aim of finding as many similarities as they can.
3 At a certain point (i.e. when they have found five similarities, or after ten minutes) ask them to look at the two pictures and see what other similarities they can find.

NOTES

This activity simply turns the very much used 'Spot the difference' (e.g. Ur 1981, pp. 51–58) on its head.

VARIATIONS

You can make the activity more or less simple by your choice of pictures. Initially the image type can be varied (e.g. black and white photo vs colour drawing); then the subject matter alters the level of the activity (i.e. it is plainly more difficult to find similarities between a picture of barren moorland and one of a packed stadium during a football match than it is between the same packed stadium and a picture showing the inside of a busy factory). You must decide what is appropriate for the different groups of learners that you teach.

6.1

LEVEL
Intermediate +

TIME
20 minutes

FOCUS
Describing; understanding an oral description

VISUALS
Dissimilar pairs of pictures; one pair for each pair of learners

6.2

LEVEL
Lower
intermediate +

TIME
30–45 minutes

FOCUS
Describing places;
understanding a
description which is
read out

VISUALS
Enough similar
pictures of bridges
for every learner in
the class to have a
different one

OTHER MATERIALS
White postcards; Blu-
tac

WHICH IS MY BRIDGE?

Procedure

1 Ask the learners to sit as far away from each other as possible.
2 Give each of them a white postcard, and allow them all to select a picture of a bridge which they do not show to anyone else.
3 Tell them that they are staying in a hotel, and that the picture is the view from their bedroom window. They are to write the postcard, describing the view in detail.
4 The learners – in secret – write their postcards; as the first ones are finishing, start collecting the pictures from all the learners. Blu-tac the pictures to the wall, very close together.
5 When everyone has finished, invite the learners to come and sit very close around the pictures, bringing their postcards with them.
6 They take it in turns to read out their postcards, while the others try to decide which picture is being described.

NOTES

a The success of this activity depends upon two key factors:
   i that no learner knows what another learner's picture is
   ii that many of the bridge pictures are sufficiently similar to cause dispute and discussion when the descriptions are read out.
b It is always an interesting moment when the pictures are displayed on the wall and the learners realise that all the pictures are of bridges!
c The activity assumes that the basic skill of landscape description has already been taught.

VARIATIONS

1 You might like to write something on the postcards to start the learners off, e.g.
   Dear ...
   We arrived at our hotel yesterday; it's very comfortable and the view from our room is lovely, etc.
2 You could write the name of another learner in the class on the postcard (*Dear Pietro*) so that when you reach Stage 6, the person to whom the card is addressed reads out the description. (NB In my experience, the difficulty of reading another learner's handwriting can sometimes break down the flow of the activity if it is done in this way.)
3 At Stage 4 you may add several other very similar pictures which have not been described. This is especially appropriate for small groups (ten or less) and for more advanced classes, as it increases the difficulty.
4 The pictures do not have to be of bridges; they may be of any other suitable landscape feature (farmhouses, bays, lakes, valley, etc.) of which you have sufficient pictures.

MATCH THE DESCRIPTION

Procedure

LEVEL
Lower
intermediate +

TIME
10–15 minutes

FOCUS
Understanding a
description

VISUALS
As many different
small (5 × 5 cm)
portrait photographs
as there are learners
in the class

**OTHER
MATERIALS**
A short paragraph
describing each
picture

1 Give each learner a picture and a non-matching description; tell them not to show anyone else either the portrait or the description.
2 Ask the learners to get up and move around the room reading the description they have and listening to other descriptions, trying to find the one which matches their picture.
3 When they hear what they believe to be the correct description, they take that card and give the description they have to the other person, whether it is the one that person needs or not.
4 They then check, by reading; if they still believe it to be the correct one they come to you for confirmation. If it isn't, they carry on.

NOTES

a Stress that learners should not show each other their descriptions and portraits, otherwise the activity loses its communicative basis.
b It is vital to emphasise that learners must have two elements (picture + description) in their hands at all times; this usually needs re-emphasising once they start exchanging descriptions.
c The cards need to be coded for ease of checking at Stage 4; I have found that if one uses a simple system (e.g. portrait A = description 1) the learners will often spend their time looking for the code! I use a system of geometrical shapes (A = ■; B = ▲; C = ●; D = ★, etc.).
d Have something else ready for those who finish first (e.g. write a description of a relative, based on the model on the card).
e At the end of the activity there are usually a few learners left who have been unable to match their pictures. Stand them in a circle and ask one learner to read out their description while the others all look at their pictures. It usually becomes obvious to them after one or two readings; if not, then you can help (e.g. *He said 'grey hair' – who has a picture of someone with grey hair?*). The last two will merely have to exchange description cards, but be sure to get them to check.
f This idea was first presented in 'Matching Activities' (Hill 1982).

VARIATIONS

1 The activity works just as well using pictures and descriptions of landscapes, technical equipment, houses, etc.
2 A simpler way of matching is to give half the class pictures and the other half descriptions, and ask them to find their partner by using the same process. This is much quicker, and easier on resources (i.e. you need half the number of pictures and descriptions) and may be more appropriate to teachers with very large classes.
3 You can give learners a picture (secretly) and ask them to write their own descriptive paragraph; these can then be used in the activity.
4 The difficulty of the task can be increased by using very similar portraits/pictures (e.g. all of grey-haired old men with glasses).

6.4

WHO DID I DESCRIBE?

LEVEL
Lower
intermediate +

TIME
10–15 minutes

FOCUS
Describing and
understanding a
spoken description of
a face

VISUALS
One set for each
learner (pair of
learners) of five to
ten very similar
portraits, of which
two must be identical

Procedure

1 Ask the learners to get into pairs (or pairs of pairs).
2 Give Learner A (Pair A) between five and ten similar portraits (e.g. seven middle-aged women with short grey hair); give Learner B (Pair B) a portrait picture which is identical to one of the pictures in the set. Tell the learners that they must not show their pictures to each other.
3 Ask the Learner B's to give a description of the person in their portrait. Learner A's should listen and ask for clarification if necessary. This should continue until Learner A knows who is being described. They may then compare cards.
4 The pair should then exchange pictures with a neighbouring pair and do the activity again the other way round (i.e. Learner A describes, Learner B listens and asks).

NOTES

a The activity can be made more secret by giving Learner A a folder to put the pictures in.
b Sets of pictures may be made permanent by sticking them into a folder, although this means that they lose their flexibility and can be only used for this activity.

VARIATIONS

The activity works just as well with pictures and descriptions of landscapes, technical equipment, houses, etc.

LANDSCAPE INTO WORDS

Procedure

1 Ask the learners to draw a suitably shaped frame (a square or rectangle usually) on a clean piece of paper, and explain that you are going to describe a view which they are going to draw.
2 Describe the picture, pausing as necessary, and repeating and reformulating as often as required, until they have finished.
3 Show the learners the original, and ask them to discuss with a partner any differences between what they have drawn and the original picture.

NOTES

a This exercise is, in fact, a type of dictation. It has immediate strong feedback, i.e. *The better I understood what was said, the closer my drawing was to the original.*
b It is important to stress at Stage 1 that you do not want a work of art (*But I can't draw!* is the most frequent response to the explanation of the activity), but simply the right things in the right places.
c The description is probably best given half in geometrical terms, and half in 'landscape' terms, e.g.
First of all draw a square with sides about 8 cm long – no, you don't need to measure it! – just get it roughly square. Now, draw a horizontal line across the middle of the square, from left to right – or from right to left if you prefer! Next, draw another line about one third of the way up from the bottom – another horizontal line one third of the way up from the bottom – under the first line you drew. The space between those two lines is the sea. Now I want you to draw a house – a low, one-storey house – in the middle of the lower line; a low house which takes up the central third – more or less – of the second line you drew . . . and so on.
This is the way I start off one of the pictures which I often use for this purpose; note the quantity of repetition and reformulation as well as banter, which all give the learners time to absorb the message. It is a good idea to practise (with a guinea-pig, if possible) before doing the activity with the class.
d This activity was first presented in my article 'Landscape into words' (Hill 1984).

VARIATIONS

The activity works well with learners dictating a description to each other, either in pairs or small groups. The only constraint is having enough suitably simple view pictures.

6.5

LEVEL
Lower intermediate +

TIME
15 minutes

FOCUS
Understanding a spoken description of a landscape

VISUALS
A picture of a view; it should be uncomplicated, and able to be described in terms of a few broad lines and shapes.

CHAPTER 7

Reading

In many ways, looking at pictures and reading are very similar, and as such, mutually exclusive; they may both be used as the starting point for other work (e.g. discussions: Section 1.5), and they may both be used as illustrations of ideas (e.g. essay writing: Section 1.2). Usually, visuals illustrate elements of a written passage, thus making the reading easier (e.g. in teaching literature: Section 1.4). This is especially so where there is a culturally-based difficulty in comprehension (e.g. cultural background: Section 1.6). On the other hand, reading can help the understanding of visuals, for example, in the catalogue notes to an art exhibition. However, it is difficult to find activities in which the use of visuals alone helps further reading skills; in fact the use of illustrations to aid comprehension of difficult lexical items in texts actually works against the development of good reading habits by rendering unnecessary the use of written context to work out meaning.

Reading has formed an important element in several of the techniques presented here (particularly *Reading their own writing*: Chapter 5, Activity 5.1, but also all the other activities in Chapter 5, as well as Chapter 6, Activities 6.2 and 6.3).

TEXT INTO PICTURES

Procedure

1 Ask the learners to get into pairs (or groups of three or four). Give everyone a copy of the same short poem and ask them to read through it several times to try and get the 'feel' of it.

2 Give each pair (group) a large pile of small pictures, and ask them to work together to try and 'translate' the poem into a visual form. You should point out that they don't need to find pictures for function words (unless they really want to!), but should concentrate on the main images. Several connected words may be put into the same image, for example, if the text being studied were Blake's 'The sick rose', the phrase 'the invisible worm' could be represented by one picture, or by two – one for 'invisible' and one for 'worm'.

3 When they have finished, they should circulate, and read back the text using each others' picture sequences.

NOTES

a It is important to choose suitable texts for this activity; short poems like Blake's 'The sick rose' are ideal, both in length and language, as the images are very powerful, but not so concrete as to be unrepresentable in other ways; the poem contains sixteen images in thirty-four words.

b The pictures should be carefully selected; there should be no concrete representations of the images used in the poem (i.e. not just no roses, for the Blake poem, but also no flowers). The best sort of visuals to use are those 'moody' pictures with a strong emotional pull (windy moorlands, desolate buildings, mossy rocks, etc.)

c Allow the learners to leave spaces for images which they do not feel able to represent from the pile of pictures they were given. Later, they can be allowed to go and borrow from other pairs (groups), or from a central bank of pictures.

7.1

LEVEL
Intermediate +

TIME
45 minutes

FOCUS
Vocabulary in poetry – increasing the feeling for words, reason-giving

VISUALS
A large number of very different small (5 × 5 cm) pictures, which preferably do not include any objects, actions, etc. mentioned in the text to be studied, a pile for each pair group

OTHER MATERIALS
Copies of the poem to be studied

7.2

LEVEL
Intermediate +

TIME
30 minutes

FOCUS
Discussing the
impact of poems on
readers; revision

VISUALS
A large selection of
large 'moody'
pictures covering as
wide a range of
images as possible

PICTURES INTO TEXT

Procedure

1 Ask the learners to choose one of the poems which they have studied during the year and particularly enjoyed; this should be a personal decision.
2 Give the learners access to the visual materials and time to look through them at leisure.
3 When they find a picture which they feel 'sums up' their poem, they should go back to their place and read through the poem, and check that it really is what they want. If it isn't, they may change it.
4 When all, or most, are satisfied with the picture they have chosen, they should take it in turns to hold up their pictures, while the other learners make suggestions (with reasons) about which poem it represents.
5 Finally the learner should explain the reasons for choosing the poem, if these have not already been realised.

NOTES

a It is important to tell the learners not to disclose which poem they choose until Stage 5, otherwise a lot of useful discussion will be cut out.
b This is a very good way of revising themes and poems at the end of the academic year, especially if there is an examination ahead.

VARIATIONS

You may tell the learners which poem they must find an illustration for, secretly telling groups of three or four learners the same poem. At the end of the exercise, when they all have a picture, you can put them into groups of those illustrating the same poem, to discuss their choices and reasons; the groups can be asked to decide which of the pictures they feel best illustrates the poem. This can then be discussed at a whole-class level.

CHAPTER 8

Warm-ups and ice-breakers

In some ways, the use of visuals works against the very concept of a warm-up as a quick, easy-to-organise activity to get the class ready for the language work to follow. 'Fast naming', a technique already descri-bed (see 'Naming': Section 1.9), is one activity which can be used. There are a few others. The same is true for ice-breakers.

A-B-C

Procedure

1 As the learners enter the classroom, give each of them a picture.
2 As soon as they are sitting down, explain that they each have a picture showing an object starting with a different letter of the alphabet from everyone else. They should shout out the name of their object in order.
3 To start, say *Who is going to start?*; once the first learner has said *Apple* (or whatever) it should be self-continuing.

NOTES

a Obviously the learners need to have learnt the English alphabet before doing this activity!
b For difficult letters (X,Z) you could supply something yourself (Xylophone, Zebra, for example), holding up a picture as you do so.

VARIATIONS

You can get the learners to come out and make a line in order as they say their word, and go all the way through, saying all the words together, when you have finished.

8.1

LEVEL
Beginner

TIME
5 minutes

FOCUS
Warm-up; revision of alphabet

VISUALS
Pictures of objects starting with different letters of the alphabet, which are known to the learners; one for each learner

8.2

LEVEL
Beginner +

TIME
5 minutes maximum

FOCUS
Warm-up

VISUALS
A single large (30 ×
20 cm) picture of
usual things in
unusual
juxtaposition

FLASH A PICTURE

Procedure

1 Keep the picture behind your back, then 'flash' it across the learners' sight-lines, and ask *What did you see?*
2 As the learners give more answers – mostly single words and short phrases – you can elicit more detail before flashing the picture again, e.g.

LEARNERS:	. . . a shoe . . .
TEACHER:	What sort of shoe?
LEARNERS:	. . . a woman's shoe . . .
TEACHER:	What sort of woman's shoe?
LEARNERS:	It's white.
TEACHER:	Yes. What else . . . ?
LEARNERS:	It's got a high heel.

3 Once all the main elements of the picture have been elicited from the learners, through language (as in Stage 2) or by increasingly long showings of the picture, then you should show them the picture for them all to enjoy and understand. At this point you may elicit any other details not brought out before.

NOTES

a This is an excellent warm-up activity, especially for the first lesson of the day, or in the situation where the learners have come from other classes (maths, chemistry, mother tongue, for example) and simply need to get switched into English for their short lesson. The elicitation of single words and short phrases is both dynamic and motivating, as well as human, for an entry into the language lesson. Compare the oft-repeated 'friendly' beginnings to classes, where learners are asked such non-textbook questions as *What did you do last night?*, thus having to move from *logarithms* to *I went out with my friends*, taking care over tenses.
b The selection of the right kind of picture is very important here; in my experience, pictures with two or three main colours and a couple of large objects are most successful. The ones which I most frequently use, for example, show:
 i a woman's high-heeled white sandal on top of an open grand piano;
 ii a razor and a peach on a glass surface;
 iii a man's wrist and cuff, wristwatch showing, horizontally across the back of part of a woman's long golden hair.
 The images are simple, the items known (when seen clearly) but are seen in abnormal close-up, location and angle.
c I first saw this technique demonstrated by Harley Brookes (then ELO, The British Council, Milan) during a seminar at Centro di Lingue Moderne, Trento, in 1978.

MARIA'S A SPOON

Procedure

1 Ask the learners to stand in a circle (or several circles if there are more than fifteen), and give each of them a different picture.
2 The first learner then says what they have and what their name is; this is repeated by the other learners, e.g.

MARIA: My name's Maria. This is a spoon.
LEARNERS: Maria's a spoon.

3 This then continues until all the learners have said what they are.
4 The group should then attempt to go right around the circle, looking just at the pictures held by the learners, saying the name and the object together. If they cannot remember, the individual can remind them (of either the object or the name).

NOTES

a This is a good way of learning each others' names quickly, and is particularly useful on short courses.
b It is a good idea to quickly and privately check that the learners know the name of the object they have a picture of, to avoid later difficulties.

8.3

LEVEL
Lower
intermediate +

TIME
5–10 minutes

FOCUS
Ice-breaker;
vocabulary of
everyday objects

VISUALS
Enough pictures of
single everyday
objects for the
learners to have one
each

8.4

LEVEL
Lower
intermediate +

TIME
5–10 minutes

FOCUS
Ice-breaker, talking
about yourself

VISUALS
A large bank of very
different large (30 ×
20 cm) pictures,
especially of the
'moody' type

TALKING POINT

Procedure

1 As learners assemble for the first session, direct them to the resource bank of pictures, and ask them to select one which they can most easily 'identify' with.
2 Once they all have pictures, ask them to mingle with each other and talk about the pictures they have chosen and why; the listeners should ask questions for clarification.
3 They should move around and meet as many of the group as possible.

NOTES

a This is a fine ice-breaker, and gets learners to a surprisingly deep understanding of each other in a comparatively short time.
b Don't worry if you hear them not talking about the pictures; the idea is to get strangers talking.

I LIKE/I DON'T LIKE

Procedure

1 As the learners assemble for the first time, ask them to select four small pictures from the large resource bank. They should choose:
   - an object they like
   - an object they dislike
   - an activity they like
   - an activity they dislike
2 When all the learners have four pictures, they should circulate and show each other what they have chosen, and talk about their choices. The listeners should ask questions for clarification.

NOTES

a There need to be lots of double pictures in the bank, especially of those things people commonly like and dislike, to allow for similarities in the learners.

b Don't worry if they are not talking about the pictures, or their likes and dislikes; the activity is successful if they are really talking to each other.

VARIATIONS

This activity can be continued beyond its ice-breaking phase by asking the learners to get together in a group with people who like (or dislike) the same object (or activity). This involves lots of discussion of grouping and reason-giving.

8.5

LEVEL
Lower intermediate +

TIME
20 minutes

FOCUS
Ice-breaker; talking about likes and dislikes

VISUALS
A large selection of small (5 × 5 cm) pictures of objects and actions

Bibliography

Alexander, LG 1965 *Essay and Letter Writing* Longman

Arnold, J 1968 *The Shell Book of Country Cards* John Baker

Baddock, B 1983 *Press Ahead* Pergamon

Baddock, B 1984 *Scoop* Pergamon

Brumfit, C and Carter, R 1986 *Literature and Language Teaching* OUP

Byrne, D 1978 *Materials for Language Teaching* **2***: Interaction Package B* Modern English Publications

Byrne, D 1967 *Progressive Picture Compositions* Longman

Byrne, D 1976 *Wall Pictures for Language Practice* Longman

Byrne, D and Rixon, S 1979 *Communication Games* NFER-Nelson

Byrne, D and Wright, A 1974 *What do you Think? 1 and 2* Longman

Carter, R and Long, M 1987 *The Web of Words* CUP

Corder, SP 1963 A Theory of Visual Aids in Language Teaching *English Language Teaching Journal* **17** (2)

Duff, B and Shindler, R 1984 *Language and Style in the Press* Collins

Gower, R and Pearson, M 1986 *Reading Literature* Longman

Heaton, JB 1975 *Beginning Composition Through Pictures* Longman

Hill, DA 1984 Landscape into Words *Modern English Teacher* **11** (3) Spring

Hill, DA 1982 Matching Activities *Modern English Teacher* **10** (2) Winter

Hill, DA 1986 Son et lumiere: Surrogate Experience as Input *Yugoslav English Language Teaching Review* **9**

Hill, DA 1985 Variations on Kim's Game *Modern English Teacher* **12** (4)

Horner, D 1984 Play the Game! *Modern English Teacher* **12** (1) Autumn

Land, G 1975 *What's in the News?* Longman

Maley, A and Duff, A 1978 *Drama Techniques in Language Learning* CUP

Maley, A, Duff, A and Grellet, F 1980 *The Mind's Eye* CUP

Matthews, A, Spratt, M and Dangerfield, L 1985 *At the Chalkface* Edward Arnold

McGrath, I 1981 *Picture Pack* Edward Arnold

Mercer, D (ed.) 1986 *The Sunday Times Book of the Countryside* Macdonald

Morgan, J and Rinvolucri, M 1983 *Once Upon a Time* CUP

Ur, P 1981 *Discussions that Work* CUP

Further reading

Buckby, M and Wright A 1981 *Picture Flashcards: Materials for Language Teaching 4* Modern English Publications

Byrne, D 1978 Materials for Language Teaching **1** (3) Modern English Publications

Byrne, D 1981 *Roundabout Picture Book* Modern English Publications

Byrne, D and Rixon, S 1979 *Communication Games* pp. 16–17 NFER-Nelson

Byrne, D and Wright A 1977 *Say What you Think* Longman

Fletcher, M and Birt, D 1979 *Newsflash!* Edward Arnold

Fletcher, M and Birt, D 1983 *Storylines* Longman

Frank, C, Rinvolucri, M and Berer, M 1982 *Challenge to Think* pp. 11–16 OUP

Geddes, M and McAlpin, J 1978 Communication Games **2** In Holden, S (ed.) *Visual Aids for Classroom Interaction* pp. 54–55 Modern English Publications

Hadfield, J 1987 *Advanced Communication Games* Nelson

Hadfield, J 1984 *Communication Games* Nelson

Heaton, JB 1966 *Composition through Pictures* Longman

Heaton, JB 1986 *Writing through Pictures* Longman

Hill, DA 1983 On Making Drills More Communicative by Using Picture Cues. In *Papers III* pp. 9–13 Department of English, Nis University

Hill, DA 1984 Reading Their Own Writing *Yugoslav English Language Teaching Review* **5** p. 37

Holden, S (ed.) 1978 *Visual Aids for Classroom Interaction* Modern English Publications

Holme, R 1985 Intuiting a Picture. In Sion, C (ed.) *Recipes for Tired Teachers* p. 15 Addison-Wesley

Maley, A and Duff, A 1983 *Drama Techniques in Language Learning* pp. 115–116 CUP

McAlpin, J 1980 *The Magazine Picture Library* Heinemann

O'Neill, R 1976 *Interaction* Longman

Retter, C and Neus, V 1984 *Bonanza* Longman

Rixon, S 1983 *Fun and Games* Macmillan

Salter, D 1985 Impressionistic Writing from Pictures. In Sion, C (ed.) *Recipes for Tired Teachers* p. 21 Addison-Wesley

Sion, C (ed.) 1985 *Recipes for Tired Teachers* Addison-Wesley

Wright, A. 1976 *Visual Materials for the Language Teacher* Longman